LEARNING ORGANIZATIONAL BEHAVIORAL STRATEGIES

JOHN LOK

Copyright © John Lok
All Rights Reserved.

This book has been published with all efforts taken to make the material error-free after the consent of the author. However, the author and the publisher do not assume and hereby disclaim any liability to any party for any loss, damage, or disruption caused by errors or omissions, whether such errors or omissions result from negligence, accident, or any other cause.

While every effort has been made to avoid any mistake or omission, this publication is being sold on the condition and understanding that neither the author nor the publishers or printers would be liable in any manner to any person by reason of any mistake or omission in this publication or for any action taken or omitted to be taken or advice rendered or accepted on the basis of this work. For any defect in printing or binding the publishers will be liable only to replace the defective copy by another copy of this work then available.

2018 Oct Print Published
All rights reserved. This book or any portion thereof may not be reproduced or used in any manner
whatsoever without the express written permission of the publisher except for the use of brief quotations in
a book review or scholarly journal

Contents

Preface

Introduction

This book divides three part : labor and consumer and organizatioal behavioral strategy. This book part first is concerned how to apply behavioral psychology method to predict labor psychology and solve labor argument challenges in societies.

This book first part is suitable to any economists or policy makers or individual consumption makers or students or businessmen who have interest to learn how to apply behavioural economy methods to judge to do the most reasonable or the most right economic activities to achieve economic benefit in everyday life. In my this book, the main important aim, I give examples to explain how to apply psychological and behavioral economic both view point related methods to raise labor

This book second part is concerned how to apply behavioral economy method to predict consumer behavior. Also I shall compare to explain what advantages and disadvantages between any one of my solvable suggestions and the any one of the company's choice of solvable method to these any one sample industry consumer behavioral economic challenges to aim to let any reader to judge whether how to choose the solvable method is better. In, conclusion, this book can provide sample industries to let students to learn how to behavioral economy method to predict consumer behaviors.

In part two, I shall indicate underground train and Disney entertainment theme park and University and unground train transportation and environmental protection businessmen etc. enterprises to explain how which can apply psychological methods to predict which client's preferable behavioral choice to achieve economic benefits more easily. Thus, if company or individual businessman can predict labour psychology or client psychologic consumption behavior. Then, which can have more confidence to attract more clients or reduce labour turnover. This book is suitable to any economists or policy makers or individual consumption makers or students or businessmen who have interest to learn how to apply behavioural economy methods to judge to do the most reasonable or the most right economic activities to achieve economic benefit in everyday life.

I shall explain how to apply behavioral economy method to attempt to predict how any consumer individual consumption of decision. How to predict why the consumer chooses to do whose consumption behavior in psychological view point. I shall introduce the different kinds of behavioral consumption of prediction methods include: the standard economic model of behavioral consumption of prediction method, online psychological advertising of prediction method, brand image attention of behavioral consumption of prediction method, store atmosphere environment influence prediction method, knowledge of the factors prediction method, constructive consumer choice processes influence prediction method, survey research prediction method ,consumer neuroscientific research prediction method etc. different psychological research of consumption methods. In second part, the main important aim, I give examples to explain how to apply psychological and behavioral economic both view point related methods to predict consumer individual behavior to let businessmen learn how to choose the reasonable or right methods to attract consumers to choose to buy whose products or consume whose services to win competitors more easily.

This book part three provide good marketing strategies for first year science business administration students to study. I write this book which concerns sample of large companies case studies. I shall apply marketing theoretical bases which are often borrowed from the disciplines of economics and psychology to give opinions to solve these large companies' problems. Practical application of theory is provided through case studies. This book tries not to present prescriptive solutions to marketing problems, but encourages discussion about causes and effects.

This book part three is arranged in four thematic discussion. The first discussion begins by identifying the fundamental building blocks of marketing. The second thematic discussion focuses on consumers, and on understanding the complex factors that lead to buying decisions. The third thematic discussion focuses on how these sample companies use knowledge about consumers and the broader marketing environment to develop a competitive advantage. The final thematic discussion seeks to integrate the previous chapters and provides an overview of the marketing management process in the context of an increasingly globalized marketing environment. I shall indicate these sample large companies, such as Body Shop, Ryanair airline, Walt Mark food supermarket , Nestle , England NHS public hospital etc. which had encountered what problems had cause difficulties to compete to their competitors as well as I shall recommend what solutions are the best to let them to solve these problems. Thus, these problems were the fact that these sample large companies had encountered. You can learn some marketing strategies to solve your business problems after you studies this book.

This book three part is arranged in four thematic discussion. The first discussion begins by identifying the fundamental building blocks of marketing. The second thematic discussion focuses on consumers, and on understanding the complex factors that lead to buying decisions. The third thematic discussion focuses on how these sample companies use knowledge about consumers and the broader marketing environment to develop a competitive advantage. The final thematic discussion seeks to integrate the previous chapters and provides an overview of the marketing management process in the context of an increasingly globalized marketing environment. I shall indicate these sample large companies, such as Body Shop, Ryanair airline, Walt Mark food supermarket , Nestle , England NHS public hospital etc. which had encountered what problems had cause difficulties to compete to their competitors as well as I shall recommend what solutions are the best to let them to solve these problems. Thus, these problems were the fact that these sample large companies had encountered. You can learn some marketing strategies to solve your business problems after you studies this book.

key words: Corporate social responsibility , marketing oriented sales oriented, production oriented, ecological concerns , ethnographic research ,cognitive information processing, demographic segmentation

Prologue

BRIEF CONTENTS

How to apply psychological method to predict consumption of behaviors

How to apply behavioral economic principles to assist policy makers
Analysis whether behavioral economy and psychology which has close relatonship.
How can consumer debt management psychological factors influence consumption behavior?
Can price change influence consumer behavior?
How can constructive consumer choice processes influence consumption behavior?
How can economical environment factor predict consumers consumption?
How can auctions or online experimentation respond to predict consumer behavior and sale forecast accuracy?
Apply knowledge management method to predict Walt Disney entertainment theme park behavioral consumption

Brand image attention of behavioral consumption of prediction method
Can scientific research method predict Disney visitors behavior ?
Can intentions Disney visitor behavior be predicted by survey research ?
Can food consumption for trust cooperation influence family or friend Disney client group ?

6.2 University campus choice and teaching method choice psychological prediction
University campus location factor
The resource based theory of university
location competitive advantage
The factor of student demand for
alternative modes of course delivery
Whether online and hybrid courses will
influence to university students to choose
the university to study.

6.3 How to predict passenger individual consumption choice for airline industry

How can airline gas or oil price influence passenger individual airline choice?

What is the relationship of oil price and terrorism to airline industry to influence ticket price increasing?

How can demand be caused by e-service transaction channel to predict passenger individual consumption choice for airline industry?

Can advertising influence consumption behavior?

How can airline atmosphere environment influence traveller travel choice behavior?

How can airline counter servicer knowledge influence traveller consumption behavior?

In -store consumer digital signage behavior how can influence consumer behavior

6.4 How does MTR (Mass Train Railway) need to consider route design location of choice?

Introduction

Why MTR underground train transportation needs to know passenger behaviour

Why route choice can influence passenger behavioural choice

Why trip time reliability and crowding factors can influence MTR passenger choice.

How to apply online psychological advertising method to predict passenger behavioral consumption?

Does habit strength moderate the intention behavior to consumption?

6.5 Why environment protection product businessmen need to concern what the degree of quality of life to their potential buyers

How environmental risk factor can influence different groups

How Afria country environmental pollution influences

How human adult consumption and environmental quality influences future environment for human survival probability of life expectancy.

Why social and physical environmental factors have close relationship to influence economic growth

How environmental factor can influence any country's house price.

How environmental pollution can influence social welfare

What is consumer neuroscientific research method to predict consumer behavior?

Whether design factor can predict consumer behavior for environment protection product

Why environmental pollution and human right abuses has close relationship to influence quality of life and economic growth?

What is space and environmental technology?

Why does environment protective product need survey to enquire design questions?

Can implicit design questionnaire (survey) or /and interview methods can test consumer behavior for measuring consumer response to environment protection product?

Raising labor effort strategy

CHAPTER ONE

Knowledgeable Jobs

Why does online knowledgeable jobs will be raised productivity ?

In what way has globalization affected employers choose online work to provide to local or overseas to raise productivity? Is online work still a useful working place environment for local and overseas employers to raise productivity in a globalized online age, such as online electronic books' authors, online office administration or online surveys or online researchers etc. kind of online jobs supplying? Our age is entering an online business environment, such as online electronic air tickets sale, online electronic books publishing, online advertising and online shopping and website design service promotion , online university education etc. different kind of online businesses from internet. It seems online channel can increase global online job chances to affect that our live and our job nature to be changed every day. For example, online electronic book publishing business will be popular, many different countries' readers who like to buy electronic books to study, due to these online electronic book shops, e.g. Amazon, lulu, book Rix, book tango etc. electronic book stores which can provide free charge to deliver cheaper paper books to any overseas countries' readers' homes and which paper book prices are more cheaper to compare to book shops' paper books process after who have paid to buy any electronic books or paper books from these online book stores websites. Moreover, these readers can read these book stores' electronic books from online publishing sellers' websites to download these electronic books to study at homes or any libraries etc. computer provision of places easily and conveniently. So readers do not need to walk to any book shops to buy any paper books and who also do not need to bring any heavy paper books back to homes conveniently. Hence, electronic publishers can provide electronic book authors' job chances to write their books and type to computers to register to be online authors to publish whose electronic or paper books to earn loyalty income at home very easily. Also, the globalizing online job nature can change the customized office work style. It won't need staffs go to office to work from 9:00 AM to 6:00 PM. In general office workers need to spend eight to ten working hours with five or six working days within per week commonly. Hence, online office workers don't need to pay transportation fee and lunch cost, due who can work at their home when who turn on their computer to enter whose employers' websites to work and make email communication to connect between them conveniently. So, I feel the online electronic book authors and online office administration jobs which will be popular further occupations to be provided from global online job structure style and many labors will like to work online, then who can raise productivity conveniently when who work at home in the future. Beside, due to online (internet) is very popular and cheap cost to be needed to spend expenditure from employer. So, internet will build the relationships between workplaces and every staff role identity and everyday life and online working environments can connect them to work in the process of globalization in the future. Also, our everyday life and work is entering in a globalizing world. It emphasizes on time and space compression and the importance of virtual space and experience in our daily lives of many people, the working style seems spent online working time to change how our social traditional work roles and our traditional office working places-based environments to home online working environments further long time in the future. So, employers ought plan to prepare online working methods to let their employees to raise productivity.

Why does knowledgeable online jobs will raise economic growth?

Social science can explain knowledgeable jobs will be useful and popular and assisting labors to raise productivity to work at home online working environments. Within social science, in such discipline is sociology and human psychology and geography which indicates internet technology have changed to online working place environment, sense of working place, online employee role identity, everyday online work and life style, website global working communication and email online communication working interconnections. It seems internet brings access to social, economic and political resources to effect change to both individual and social working conditions, such as employers accept to attempt to use internet to assist office staffs to work at home, e.g. many book publishing businesses like to attempt to publish electronic books from online book store, instead of book shops channel to sell paper books. So these online book stores give chance to authors to publish electronic books or online paper books from online sale channel to earn loyalty income. For example, Amazon online electronic bookstore can publish electronic books and online paper books to sell all one day 24 hours to any countries' readers from its website, so when any countries' readers can enter its website to choose any different kind of subjects of electronic books to buy by visa card conveniently. Such as fiction, psychology, economy, science, law, architecture, medicine, commerce, management etc. subjects. So, any country's reader who does not need to buy air tickets to go to the country's book shop to buy the paper book, who only needs to pay visa card to buy the electronic or online paper books from Amazon publishing's website to buy any countries' electronic and paper books and then the overseas reader can choose either to download it from whose home computer or pays more price to deliver the online paper book to post to whose country conveniently. Hence, this online bookstore sale method will be popular and many free work authors will choose to work to raise the productivity of more quality electronic books numbers from this internet channel. However, the consequences of global change are far from uniform with globalizing influences and adapted as new technological, economic and online working cultural experiences are incorporated by any countries' staffs of any cities, towns and rural areas into their everyday work lives from long distance easily. Since one company can employ different countries' staffs to work from internet working channel at their homes. For example, a America company can employ overseas countries' staffs to work at the same time together by sending job duties from email communication channel among them when the America company has any job arrangement to notify to any staff to finish it any time, then the overseas staff finish the job and who can send whose finished documents to whose America employer any time. It seems the overseas staffs whose working hours can be flexible and those working hours have no regular office working hours to be fixed time table, so they do not need to work in any fixed working time table every working days, who can send their finished office documents to whose employers after who have finished their documents by either email communication channel or office online website downloads office download any time conveniently.

It will be a new working style position that online working globalization is in a new stage. We are living in an age of very rapid and fluid flow of information, ideas, products and people which are having an effect of a variety of scales. I shall indicate evidences to explain why employers will encounter online knowledgeable jobs to raise productivity in a globalizing world by sociology concept. I shall focus on research into the connections between our everyday online life style, online working place and online working role identity. The first is that everyday online life is the manifestation of social existence and always involves either distant or direct interaction with other people. Such as we can use internet email channel to communicate with overseas friends or strange people, even employers or employees can also use email to exchange to receive and send their office documents by email or company website any time conveniently. Good example includes such things are as online participation in work, employment, cultural events, and recreation, shopping and communication from internet channel. It is related to employees are working in whose home working places and their home working place are possible to connect their overseas employers' offices and however, readily these may be separated in far distant conceptual terms, such as an online working environment. The employee's home is such whose employer's office, who can work at home from online channel conveniently. When who receives whose employer's email about what job duties who needs to do every day. Then, who sees his employer's email, then either if who did not understand how to do whose job duties clearly, who can send email back to ask whose employers to explain how who needs to do whose office job duties by email communication channel again easily. Even after who finish whose office job duties on that day or another day, then who can send finished office job duties to whose employers by email conveniently. In this view, online working places and sense of online working places are produced by different countries' large enterprise employers and overseas employees interacting together. At the same time, employees and employers whose sense are contacted by employees' individual role identity from email or office website communication channel any time. Thus, traditional office working environment is constrained and enabled by different countries' working histories and cultures and social class backgrounds and economic conditions and job opportunities, working positions of power and working geographical locations and development of local change and distant social interaction. In the future, online working place will be changed from traditional socially significant to online social relationship; underlying this sense of online working place will be the notion that some employers and employees themselves ought feel that life. Moreover, online working place is the possibility of non controlling employees' working time, due to working hours are flexible and employers' working places sizes are very limited to supply to many staffs to work in a limited office working place in the same working time. It seems online home environment will be very popular, due to every employee will use whose home to work to finish whose office documents at home every day any time very conveniently as well as employers won't need to spend much expenditure to pay for large sizes of office rent when the employer needs to rent more than one room office at more than one floor in one building. Hence, company's website expenditure can reduce the employers' office rent seriously. Moreover, employees can be dominated by feelings towards changing general office working place to online working at home as well as changing fixed working time table to flexible working time table, e.g. the staff can see whose employer's email to know what office job duties who needs to do tonight, so who will finish whose office documents and will send whose finished office documents to whose employer by email tomorrow. So, home online working environment is seen as an ideal home working place, and home online working environment which is quiet, safe and it has certain valued facilities and home online working environment is such as the type of residents in the employee's living building. This sense of living and online work place will be held by residents who will be employed in professional/ managerial/ technical etc. occupations. Hence, local employees won't catch any transportation to go to office as well as overseas employees won't also catch planes to go to whose employer's country's office to work, due to who can use online email communication or office website communication channels to work together conveniently. However, working facilities will be one online computer working commodity which is purchasable, useable and exchangeable and saleable to any employees are located at home and employers are located at office, and after a flexible working time table is discarded easily by employer, due to whose website or office email can receive any employee's individual finished office documents by every employee's individual email communication any time very conveniently. Moreover, home online working place is also like a stage on every employee's life is lived out. The employee will feel that whose life and working time is lived at home together at the same time. Similar to feel commodity sense of home and the working place which are the same location, but it is distinguished from it by the establishment of arriving strange and far distant of the employee's local or overseas employer's office when the employee's working place is family interacting to the employee's house or home.

Our world is entering globalization, people are connecting in an increasing number of ways. It is clear also that is the face of globalization, the ways of our everyday working life is either constituted which are still shaped by local expenditure of working place or is by where the firm's overseas employees love locally, regionally and nationally or is by the access who have limited to office resources and home office online working locations opportunity changing from general office working environment to home online working environment. Roberston (1992) shows is that" this is not just about economic processes, but about social and cultural issues are as well. In the early part of the 21 ST century, it is necessary to see this as a set of processes that encompass economic, political, social, cultural and environmental changes."

Why employers need to considerate the low

income level worker whose living of standard challenge.

Is globalization influenced to new online knowledgeable jobs to be provided to raise low income level worker's living od standard? One of the key areas of debate among theorists is the extent to which globalization is a new phenomenon or stage in a process. When it began and the path that it has followed and thus how new it is. Such as internet is used in communication aspect in early, e.g. hospital or war email communication channel. Then, many businessmen discovered online electronic commerce is also one online sale and purchase method. So, it will cause online office workers or online freelance online jobs, e.g. electronic book authors working style or electronic book reading cultural existed in our society in common possibly in the future. However, I recognize globalization is a misleading concept since what is described as globalization has been happening for the 500 years history ago. Rather what is new is that human are entering an age of transition, such as online knowledgeable workers or knowledgeable nature of different jobs will be caused from online working environment popularly. There are key processes of globalization: the economic, often is seen as the central process, the political, social, cultural and online working environment. Every natural economy needs to maintain the rate of growth, employment, welfare provision and minimum wage balance levels, so it will cause knowledgeable jobs provided, such as online organized labors, it also will change the traditional office organizational environment to cause online new organizational home work environment popularly in the future. Hence, economic and political has close connection, political and cultural has also close connection, cultural and social has also close connection, social and working environment has also connection. After all these connections cause globalization finally, then the new online knowledgeable working environment, such as online jobs will be required by global office employees popularly in the future. It will bring many online workers supply to the employment market in the future. As capital in the new globalized economy has a limited attachment to working place, production centers, such as offices, factories or farms which locate any where it is competitively advantages to do so, and economic activity moves to where labor is cheapest or raw materials is the least expensive. It can be raised demand to online knowledgeable workers demand in global competitive employment environment directly. For example, cultural, social, global expansion of Mc Donald's and other fast food chains will be entered to the online sale channel. Hence, environmental globalization raises human awareness, includes a new view of the natural and the social worlds to environmental protection message. These message source is from online channel popularly nowadays. Online organizing environment and living will influence our everyday working worlds. Due to many industrial cities and life will be not needed by global employers. However, industrial cities concentrate on demanding in developing countries, e.g. China, India, Korea etc. countries. So, developed countries, such as America, England, Japan etc. countries' employers will need many online knowledgeable employees to help them to work from online work place environment popular in the future. Later, knowledgeable online working environment will be popular to developing countries when which economy had developed mature in the future. So, it is possible online jobs will raise low income level householders' living of standard.

CHAPTER TWO

LIVING STANDARD MEASURE STRATEGY

Is income a useful indicator to measure living standard to assist economic growth?

Nowadays, developing countries, such as India, China, Hong Kong, etc. and developed countries, such as America, England etc. which are facing social challenges. For example, many low income level householders whose income level can't be raised and inflation is also high in society. Although, these developing countries' economy is growing, but which can not raise the low income level householders' income level to let them have afford to buy one house in minimum in whose country, even these low income level family have no enough income to buy foods to eat and cloths to wear easily. Also, the developed countries' economy had arrived the mature growing stage, but which also can not give any benefits to whose low level income level income householders group. Hence, governments have responsibilities to find methods to solve these challenges, such as: How to reduce poor occurrence? How much does economic growth help the poor? How can social policy help? Can a country have a sizeable low-wage sector of house to provide to the poor? What role can public service social spending better for the poor?

Justice is the distribution of income and wealth is fairest. Any country's government needs play a large role in determining it's citizen's abilities to do common occupation, what job choices are preferences to them, how to raise employment of motivation and what social circumstances are to cause households have no poor occurrence to cause many low level income jobs to do to earn income in society. In order to reduce the unfair income distribution between rich and poor people. Why it is important to improve unfair income treatment between rich and poor people to any countries? However, in a rich and growing economic country, such as America, England etc. , which are difficult to justify stagnant living standards for those at the floor bottom low income people nowadays. Although, these developed countries' economy are growing, but which can not give benefits to this low level income households group. However, I suggest any country ought favor not simply a satisfactory level of living standards for the poor people, but it ought consider how to improve or review poor people living standards every year. Analysts typically set the poverty line at 50 or 60 percent of the median income within each country. In general, poverty means to level of resources insufficient to achieve a minimal acceptable standard of living as well as people tends to experience poverty as relative is to living standards by comparison in any country's citizen's own society. If the absolute incomes or living standards for the poor grow less rapidly than those of households in the middle income level in the country. So, it seems that it is not fair economic growth in these developing countries..

How to apply " standard growth enhancing policy" to
improve low income level householders living of
standard to raise productivity

Is income a useful indicator of living standards? Income is a resource that allows any country's households to acquire the sort of things e.g. food, housing, medical care, transportation, education, entertainment etc. needs. So, which are needed for a minimal decent standard of living. Income also is comparatively easy to measure. However, causing poor factors might have many reasons, such as illness, temporary unemployment, a large amount of bonus reduction, overtime long time working hours, family members unemployment, even economic decline (falling down), so these factors can reduce jobs supply to any countries to cause poor occurrence. However, any countries' income measures seldom include the value of government service and in kind benefit, such as pension, unemployment assistance etc. as well as some low income households have assets (savings in bank, and owned home). So, it seems income is not an accurate measure to the actual living standard to the low income people numbers in the countries effectively. If income is not an accurate measure to actual living standard, then it can not improve the low income level householders of living standard and productivity level will be reduced because these low income level labors can not get reasonable salaries and unfair welfare to work from whose employers. Otherwise, the high income level labors can get increased salaries and fair welfare to work from whose employers. When these both low and high income level labors work in same company, the low income level labors will feel angry to work unhappy, then it is possible that who will decrease their productivity.

The poor people numbers will be reduced possibly. How to evaluate the actual poor people numbers decreasing? In think when the degree to the country which economic growth boosts the income level of low and households to rise their general savings amounts to the income level of middle households. Then, the country's poor people numbers will be decreasing, due to this group of the numbers of incomes level of low households has been decreasing and it's numbers has been increasing to the income level of middle group, then productivity will also raise to every employers in any country.

In general, economic growth is assumed that poor households get more jobs, work more hours and/or receives higher wages. Hence, when one country measure economic growth, which can apply the relationship between per capita GDP and low income households of numbers between the past year and current year to measure the rising or falling numbers per capita GDP in the low and income households group, for example, in Sweden, Denmark,

Norway, the Netherlands and Finland countries which net transfers are received by low income level households increased significantly between 1979 year and 2007 year. But, average earnings, were flat in Demarks country, when in Sweden and Finland countries which declined sharply during those countries' deep recessions in the early 1990 year. Otherwise, in the United Kingdom, the period was from 1979 year to 1995 year, it saw no changes in transfers pension or retirement savings from United Kingdom government and a slight drop in earnings, but from 1999 year to 2005 year, social earning increased slightly, but more important was a large rise in net government pension and retirement saving transfers, which resulted in a sizeable increase in low income level incomes group. When net government pension or retirement savings transfers to citizen increased this was caused by economic growth. In general, economic growth allows policy makers to boost inflation-adjusted benefit levels for pension or retirement saving transfer to citizen programs, which will increased the incomes of pension or retirement saving benefit recipients. With GDP rising, government social benefit pension or retirement saving transfers as a share of GDP tended to remark more or less constant.

However, in some countries, the rise in pension of retirement saving net transfers was achieved in part by reduction of income or profit taxes for low income households or low business profit households, since the 1970 year, most of the world's rich nations, such as America, united Kingdom have not significantly increased the share of their GDP that goes to pensions or retirement savings transfer for the low income level poor households. It seems that if any country hoped the low income level of householders numbers will be increase, which ought need to upgrade their low income level to go up middle income level in society, then its economic growth will be raising. How economic growth can boost incomes for the poor households. It seems economic growth has made rising low income level of households is more likely, but several countries are exceptions. They experienced growing per capita GDP, but little or no improvement in the income of low income level of households, such as Hong Kong has seven million people who are living in a small city. Although, it was encountering economic growth from 1970 year in beginning, but the low income level of households had little or no improvement, it was possible that the numbers of Hong Kong low income level of households are more than the middle or high income level of households seriously. So, the HK economic growth seems not improve low income level of households to assist this low income level of households to raise whose income to be risen to the middle income level of households group. The reason is possible that the failure of some governments to increase public transfers as the economy grows is a key part of reason. But why did not more economic growth reach the low income level of poor households in the form of rising market income? For example, in HK, whether economic growth is likely to directly benefit the poor group's employment hours reduction and rising hourly wage levels. However, I discovered that HK economic growth produced no increase in the wage or salary market rate of low level of income households and without employment hours reduction and without rising hourly wage levels. So, HK economic growth seems to raise more job supply in the employment market, but it seems without employment hours reduction. Otherwise, it's economic growth rises employment hours, but without rising hourly wage. Hence, it seems low income level householders of numbers and economic growth have close relationship to any country, so employers need to concern their labors numbers of low income level to raise their income to be middle income level in society.

CHAPTER THREE

LABOR ETHIC

I recommend this economic policy to reduce poor occurrence, such as growth on average benefit the poor as much as anyone lives in the country's society, such as "standard growth enhancing policy" should be at the center of any poverty reduction strategy. I believe economic growth is the most powerful instrument for reducing poverty, due to many businessmen have enough money to invest to their countries to do any kind of businesses, then the jobs supply will be raised any many people can get any jobs supply number is more than job seekers number, then it is no doubt, the unemployment numbers will be reduced. When many people have new jobs to do and who can earn enough wages to prepare to save more money in bank.

What has been the impact of economic growth on employment hours and wages? In fact, work hours are matter a great deal for the incomes of poor group of households in developed countries, such as United States or United Kingdom or developing countries, such as Hong Kong, China etc. countries. For example, HK economic growth has a large influence to raise employment hours more than rising wage levels, such as HK general working hours are risen up to 10 to 12 hours or more per week working days to low income level of households, but the low income level of households group has not been rising wage level generally. So, I feel HK economic growth could not give any benefits to the low income level of households, such as without reduction employment hours and without raising wage level to the low income level of households in HK. Also, HK's economic growth only raises many jobs supply in HK society. Otherwise, America economic growth can give benefits to low income level of households, such as reduction employment hours, rising wage level to low income level of households and raising jobs supply in America society. Hence, the developed countries, such as America , England which economic growth can give more benefits to low income level of households. Otherwise, the developing countries, such as India, China, Korea which economic growth can not give more benefits to the low income level of households and these developing countries will cause disadvantages to this low income level of poor group in society. It is possible that the developing countries' low income level of households often need to increase to spend more working hours to assist whose employers to develop whose employers' business, due to their employers do not want to increase to employ extra workers or staffs to assist whose business development, who need whose current employees to raise more extra working hours to work to raise work efficiency when these developing countries are encountering the economic growth stage.

For example, HK employers do not concern moral issues about abnormal working hours influence. The outcome is either Hong Kong labors work long time working hours abnormally who can not rise Hong Kong economic growth or who can rise Hong Kong economic growth in long time. Generally, Hong Kong employers choose to pay less salary expenditure to need many extra labors to work abnormal working hours to help them to rise productivity, but who don't concern that long time working factor will influence unhealthy to current workers due to who need to work long time working hours abnormally in long time and it seems to cause their workers will reduce productivity and inefficiency in long time.

Although, it is possible that HK labors can be increased extra abnormal working hours to work to rise Hong Kong employers' productivity and assist HK social economy will be grown up in short term, but it is also possible that it can't rise Hong Kong economic growth due to their unhealthy or sick increasing to cause productivity declining and inefficiency in long time. Thus, I shall find evidence to analyze whether Hong Kong labors need to work abnormal long time working hours. Otherwise, who will decline Hong Kong economic growth and reduce productivity and inefficiency in long time as well as I shall give suggestion to indicate whether either current workers work abnormal long time working hours or employers ought choose to employ more extra part time workers to assist current labors to rise their productivity to decide which is the best choice to raise HK economic growth and efficient productivity in long time.

Effects on Hong Kong employment of working time reduction is found to be difficult to predict. The results of Hong Kong macroeconomic simulations of the effects on employments of working time reduction rely heavily on certain basic assumptions, such as how many hours people will actually work or how productivity and pay levels will develop. Whether HK abnormal working hours will assist HK social economic growth or economic falling down in long term.

The reasons cause Hong Kong labors who need to work abnormal long time working hours. In fact, it isn't the reason that the Hong Kong high skillful labors market is shortage to supply for the nature of some occupations, e.g. hospital doctors and nurses, university teachers, law firm lawyers etc. professional occupations. HK has many high qualification university students graduation, it has enough labor supply to high labor market every year. The reason is that employers don't like to spend more salary to increase to employ extra labors to share current workers workload, such as low skillful and hardworking labors, such as cleaners, securities, waiters and high skillful professionals, such as hospital doctors and nurses, university teachers, lawyers etc. However, the low and high skillful labor market can be enough supply in Hong Kong, but Hong Kong employers need the current high and low both skillful workers who need to work more than 10 to 12 hours or more per working day commonly. It is possible that HK high and low educational labors will be caused unhealthy and lack enough sleep if who still need to work abnormal working hours time in long time. Although, who can rise productivity and efficiency in the short time, but it is possible that who can't rise productivity and inefficiency in the long time. Moreover, it will cause many young or middle or old ages high educational or low educational knowledgeable hardworking workers who will lose many jobs provided and who will be hard to find any jobs in HK labor employment market if HK employers don't choose to pay extra salaries to employ extra full time workers to share current labors' workload in the high and low salary occupations, due to they only choose to increase abnormal additional extra working hours to current workers to achieve to reduce employment expenditure and raise productivity. Hence, it is possible to influence HK social economy grows up slowly, even it's economy can go down seriously in long time.

I shall assume that working wage or salary of every individual labors can not be increased, even can be decreased as well as whose normal working hours can be increased abnormally in generally. This means that the Hong Kong individual worker's income will be decreased and general productivity raising is not affected generally, due to HK employers need current labors to work abnormal extra working hours to attempt to raise productivity daily, but their salary or wage have not increased more. However, HK employers need many workers to accomplish the same amount of work, even who don't like to employ extra labors to assist current workers to achieve long term productivity raising in their companies. These abnormal working hours labors will feel unfair treatment, due to they need to work abnormal working hours, but their salary or wage have not been increased.

In the first scenario of my hypothesis is about that HK labor employment market's general salary or wage has not been increased to the normal proportion of the increased extra abnormal working time(hours). Then, in HK labors market, due to the numbers of labors supply is more than the jobs supply because HK employers don't like to pay more salary or wage expenditure to employ extra labor, but they like to increase extra abnormal working hours to current workers to aim to achieve productivity. So it will cause many HK job seekers with adequate qualifications or with less qualifications who won't find any jobs easily, then the HK the numbers of unemployed people will be increased and their household incomes will decrease to cause many HK household do not like to spend easily. The result will cause a negative effect on HK social private consumption will be decreased and the businessmen' income will be decreased also. So, HK people private consumption decreasing will influence HK economy growth to be slow, even it will cause HK economy declining in the long time.

In the second scenario of my hypothesis is about that Hong Kong workers are fully compensated for the increasing extra abnormal working time(hours) by the abnormal additional working hours calculation. Although, Hong Kong companies' productivity will be raised, but which are not to the extent that it compensates Hong Kong enterprises for their increased wage or salary costs. In fact, Hong Kong enterprises, their costs are passed on to the clients, it causes Hong Kong's economic growth has an impact on international competitiveness to cause economic declining in possible when these enterprises need to raise their products' sale prices to balance their salary or wage cost raising to win their import competitors. Another effect is that Hong Kong individual labor's incomes decrease, which means that Hong Kong private consumption also falls in this scenario to influence HK economic growth seriously. Thus, the HK economic growth problem will be caused, due to these factors lead to a fall in Hong Kong social household private consumption. Consequently, it will cause many HK employers hope to raise Hong Kong productivity and they will raise the total amount of Hong Kong labor actually worked hours will be risen to such as extent as the increasing in normal working time(hours) from 8 or 9 hours per normal working day to 10 or 11 or 12 hours, even more extra abnormal hours per working day to the current labors. But they do not like to spend more salary or wage expenditure to employ full time extra labors, instead of increasing extra abnormal working hours to current labors to achieve productivity of raising, due to the cost will be increased if they choose to employ extra full time labors if they want to raise productivity. However, I feel they will raise productivity in the short term, but they will not raise productivity in the long term when they choose to raise their current labors abnormal working hours per working day.

The assumption will be made regarding to the relationship between the HK labor market's abnormal long time working hours factor and whether it can influence Hong Kong economic growth in long time for this research economic problem. For example, how many hours Hong Kong labor would actually work or how much workers have efficient productivity and efficiency and how much salaries or wages would be affected as a result of the increasing in working time(hours) in Hong Kong employment market.

I shall apply endogenous growth theory to Hong Kong labor market. As this theory indicates that this model also incorporated a new concept of human capital, whose capital is increasing rates of return. Research done in this area has focused on what increases human capital (e.g. education) or technological change (e.g. innovation) to influence HK economic growth. In macro economic environment, it indicates that economic growth means the increase in the market value of the products and services produced by the country's economy over time. It is conventionally measured as the percent rate of increase in real growth domestic product or real GDP. The growth of the ratio of GDP to population (GDP per capital, per capita income). Thus, an increase in growth is caused by more efficient use of inputs is referred to as intensive growth. GDP growth is caused only be increased in such as capital, population or territory is called extensive growth. Thus, in economy growth theory, typically refers growth off potential output, i.e. production is at full employment. However, HK unemployment ratio is still high to compare other developed or developing countries, although the labors supply are enough to HK employment market.

The working time is the period of time that an individual spends at paid occupation labor. Many countries regulate the work week by law, such as minimum daily rest periods, annual holidays and a maximum number of working hours per week. Working time may vary from person to person often depending on location, cultural, lifestyle choice and the profitability of the individual's livelihood.

Generally, most Hong Kong employers need labors work long time working hours abnormally. For example, low educational workers, such as security occupations of labors need to work per working day is twelve hours or more, restaurant waiters and dish cleaners also need to work ten to twelve hours or more per working day, bank counter cashiers or audit firm staffs also need to work over time from 10 to 12 hours or more per working day and who have no extra salaries for over time salaries payment commonly. Standard working hours or normal working hours refers to the legislation to limit the working hours per day, per week, per month or per year. If an employee needs to work overtime, the employer will need to pay overtime payments to employees as required in the law. Generally speaking, standard working hours countries word wide are around 40 to 44 hours per week (but not everywhere:

such as France employers need labors work from 35 hours per week, North Korea employers need labors work up to 112 hours per week). Maximum working hours refers that the employee can't work than the level specified in the maximum working hours law. It seems that Hong Kong many employers had needed labors to work above standard working hours per week to compare to other developed countries, e.g. America, France, England, New Zealand etc. developed countries.

In conclusion, in my viewpoint, HK employers need to provide on job training to current labors to aim to raise their efficiency to productivity in the long time. Because when their labors had been trained to let them to learn how to use special skill to finish their job duties easily, then they will not need to spend much time (additional working hours) to finish their job duties per working day. On the one hand, HK employers need to measure to compare what benefits are in favor of standard working hours to whose employees. The benefits include, such as promoting work life balance and enjoy family life, increasing time for leisure and rest, beneficial to health and employees can have more time to pursue further studies as well as employers do not need to pay higher salaries to longer working hours employees or overtime pay boost income as most HK companies pay time and a half to some employees only. On the other hand, HK employers need to measure to compare what benefits are against standard working hours to employers, such as employing many part time working hours employees to assist normal working hours full time employees rather than needing full time employees work abnormal hours daily, lowering or cancelling year and bonus etc. Moreover, HK employers may also use various measure to offset the increased cost of running businesses, such as lowering average hourly annual compensation. However, when HK employees are forced to work part time jobs, who may need to acquire additional employment to maintain their standard living. Even, HK employers only force employees to work overtime in some situations. Appropriate standard working hours can vary across different industries based on the type of work performed. Such as some HK certain professional positions are difficult to define in terms of appropriate working hours. Issues can arise with employers expecting employees to work extra hours "off the clock" in order to keep costs down. Thus, I believe that HK labors abnormal working hours time issue ought be decreased and HK employers ought employ extra workers assistance to share current labors' workload to help them to raise productivity and efficiency and HK economy will grow fast in the long time. Finally, my research aims to find that the number of hours worked is a more responsive measure of the state of the labor market than employment in HK. Comparing the number of hours worked to indicators of the wider economy shows that it is likely to be demand from HK firms (employers) which is driving the numbers of hours, rather than individual job applicant supply to HK employment market. My analysis also show that the HK appears to have developed a long working hours culture to compare other developed countries, such as America, England, Canada etc. In fact, in the presence of HK firms may even invest to find which are more profitable to able to reduce their every employee's abnormal working hours daily rather than normal number of working hours of their every employee.

Finally, I shall recommend some methods to rise the living standard to low income level households group in any countries. On the income policy, I recommend governments ought implement the progressive tax policy, so the income taxes tend to be progressive to the middle and high income level of households. It aims to achieve the low income level group and the middle and high income level groups whose income level to be balanced. Whereas taxes on payroll and consumption usually are regressive, due to payroll and consumption taxes are more useful than income taxes for increasing revenues taxes on income and payroll are the least conductive to economic growth, so payroll taxes can raise growth of employment in possible. Because the low income level of households have no more effort to spend to buy any expensive products or foods generally, so who can pay less taxes when who spend less. Otherwise, because the middle or high income levels of households have more effort to spend to buy any expensive products or foods generally, so who need pay more taxes when who spend more. It is possible to reduce the level amount of difference of savings between the low income level of households and the middle income level of households. Finally, I conclude that the method of taxes on payroll and consumption usually are regressive and the method of income taxes tend to be progressive to the middle and high income level of households, which are possible to raise the low income level of households of living standard for long term if governments could attempt to achieve these two policies to apply to the low income level group and the middle income level groups both, such as income tax and payroll or consumption tax policies both. It aims to raise the better of standard of life to the low income level household and to assist the low income level household can be upgrade to the middle income level household group in the short time quickly.

Economists claim to be scientists or technicians who study fact, not values, who make scientific studies and predictions to decide why this matter is caused and to find the reasons. Often the public sector economists in USA predict the economic processes and find the facts of the world have not supported the economists' models wrongly. However, economists have ethical rules to control their behaviors to be judged any matter and to give the corrective and reasonable decisions to let public to know correctively. Hence, who can't attempt to mislead facts to present to let public to receive the wrongly message to achieve themselves unreasonable benefits and rewards. In fact, economist is similar to lawyer or accountant profession, who need to provide a "service" discipline to give corrective and reasonable judgement and facts and who can not attempt to mislead to publish whose economic research reports to let public to get wrong information frequently. I believe that the scientific of economics of the 20th century fully accepts the ethical separation. Economic theory is seen as a positive science which has to analyze and to explain the mechanisms of economic processes. Ethical valuations should not form part of the economist's research program. Modern economics stresses rational calculation, the base material objections and scientific neutrality on moral issues. I think whose idea is concerned micro economy is based on assumptions of rationally selfish behavior. Whether what is concerned to current ethical crisis in economics? Economic matters have been debated throughout human history. I feel economic ethical matters which can be concerned in aspects, such as wealth accumulation, lending, business and commerce economic issues, journals or reports or books publishing. Due to any economic matters happen in economic processes which will be recorded in history, then economists will analyze why these issues are caused and find what reasons which cause the economic issue happening is discussed by theology, ethics and politics issues are as view points. So, the moral and ethics is needed to concern to any economists when who need to do any economic research nowadays.

Economy is concerned to human will face limited resources to use or spend, so economy theory indicates to be researched what methods how human chooses to allocate resources to achieve the efficient and effective result. Economy aims to achieve human rationality to control the desire to acquire material products in order to allow better satisfaction of the true human need. Many economists concern for others now directly affects one's own welfare and commitment drives between personal choice and personal welfare and thus undermines modern economics ethic. Individuals frequently display commitment, acting against their own welfare in favor of the group. This element of ethical behavior has been ignored by economists and needs to be brought into the analysis. Although ethical motivation are relevant to economists, but the capabilities approach is more concerned with social achievement. To a large degree, this is a theory of distributive justice that economy and political science and philosophy theories which have more relationship among of these three subjects theories.

Why ethic relates to labor behavior

I shall give some current economists' judgement to indicate how well human are doing according to the capability standard to prove why employers need to concern moral behavior. The capability approaching requires that many means be provided to every person. This is an alternative to social achievement from economics approach, which uses the quantity of commodities available for consumption. The conventional measure of the standard of living (GDP/head) has been subject to sustained criticism in recent times, one source of the complaints is the capability theorists. This capabilities approach is a new inter-disciplinary social science and there are still many problems with this approach to concern ethical issues of mainstream economics. However, some economists feel that ethical motivations exist and play a role in human's actual behavior. Human well being refers to living a full human life. It measures to show the things that demonstrate a good life being lived. So, human functioning achievements, must be the focus. Possession of a certain quantity of commodities, however, may be necessary in order to achieve human functioning. This provides social success in delivering well being across our society. Moreover, some scientists who also believe the standard of social success may be limited to basic functioning. Alternatively, a rich of human group may be accepted, but social success may be considered for only a small proportion of the population. So, for each theorist, we need to ask these following questions. Does the theorist present an ethical view of motivation? Does the theorist adopt a deep mind of human well being? In the assessment of social success, does the theorist concern human functioning achievements and means to promote functioning achievements?

I shall analyze on individual psychology, household psychology and social achievement three aspects to indicate labor morality and raising productivity and even economic growth has close relationship as below:

In economic view, household means a family which has female control functioning. On the individual and public policy means that support individual achievements. However, in concept analysis, I shall indicate three levels of analysis to economic ethic of human behavior. The lowest level is individual, it is individual psychology, human functioning and ethical motivation. The middle level is household, it is household management, moral education, character formation. The highest level is the city, it is social achievement (Public policy supports equipment needs for individual capability achievement and formative law). So, human's behavioral is an assumption of modern economics. From history viewpoint, our economic conditions are largely agricultural with some mining, manufacturing and commerce, there was limited scope for domestic and international markets; mutual give and take, lending and borrowing between households was widespread. Commonly, these activities are general human economic behavior of reasons to cause these business activities in our society.

Firstly, on individual psychology aspect, human's economy of behavior is in our society, human needs do this economy behavior because human needs have good life and education, the good life required leisure and the good use of leisure time to do leisure activities with friends. Otherwise, leisure required freedom from the duties of earning a living. It was commonly accepted that the good life is required to work to earn, such as labors, traders, professions, farmers etc. service or labor occupations their individual behavior is aim to achieve earning for good life and education. So, who need to spend some time to do economic activities to aim to earn some time for leisure and education.

Secondly, on household management psychology aspect, in general, managing revenues and expenditures is a part of household management. However, household management requires moderation on the desires for food, wine, sex and sleep. So, in labor economy relationship, household seems to be the frame of mind and habits needed for engineering to make sense. In old age, expenditure on subsistence continues, but no one will pay for the labor of the old. Saving for old age, therefore is sensible. However, if one is habituated in youth to lazy, one will find it hand to change later. Nevertheless, these habits are unsustainable in old age, when one can't be labor and generate income. Hence, in labor economy view, moderation is an essential element of good household management. Although, wealth is also important, but more important is the knowledge or skill of household management. However, if one has no leisure and is unable to develop his capabilities (including bodily and non-bodily pleasures to easy to live with). Then, productivity will be reduce and inefficient work, due to the labor is hard to work, who feel himself/herself is such as a machine and who has no much time to rest often. Also the earning of friendship is also important, including certain market relationships in our modern societies. Clearly human's labor economy of behavior of household management in the broad sense is a comprehensive act and part of a way of human life. Hence, an ethical understanding is also needed, such as friendship relationship to complete household management in the middle level of household management between the city level and individual level. On functioning achievement and freedom to individual of labor economy behavior, it includes education, increased physical training etc. economic benefits to our individual in our society. Just as the city is a complex structure, so is human psychology to cause labor economy behavior. Justice in the city is defined as each class (and each individual within the class) doing its own job, justice in the individual is defined as each part of individual doing its own job. Hence, a good city has all of the individuals correctly assigned to the different classes and each individual and each class performs its appropriate job. Similarly, the good individual has each of labor's performing its job appropriately.

In the final social achievement aspect, it concerns micro. As the growth of the healthy city showed up to a certain point, economic development is required in terms of the city's physical size and population. So, modern economic principles are adopted (such as economic development and the division of labor). Nevertheless, our society must be justify to some degree to market relations. Various property rights and exchange justice must be enforced. These principles, however are limited by other ethical principles guiding the laws. Nevertheless, citizens are to be banned from engaging in most occupations. For example, the moral dangers of commercial activities are great. Moreover, market are limited to a specific location and regulated by market regulators. Although, duties are not imposed on foreign trade, prohibitions apply to various unnecessary imports and to exports of necessities. Hence, it will influence labor demand and job supply to influence the country's economic development in any time. To analyze labor economy, we need to know human nature and to establish the functions of human beings. These functions are shared with human beings, e.g. humans need to eat, drink. As a general rule, the passions that drive human to satisfy these needs, but it is of limited amount to supply. So, these factors will influence labor's behavior between action, motivation and character. However, every organization is influenced to economic growth every year by its staff individual behavior, such as its staff individual has passions and emotions disposed toward bad action and decides to act well for other reasons, e.g. the staff feels fear of detection or punishment and then who will act well because of the staff's self control to avoid the firm will dismiss him/her in the firm. It seems the staff's passion, emotion will influence whose behavior to be good or bad to do whose work in whose firm. Hence, the firm needs have economic analysis to decide to dismiss the staff or not dismiss the staff if it discovered whose behavior is not acceptable to its firm and what it will be influenced from whose bad behavior in the short term and long term. If the staff is very important and if who left this firm, this firm will face business failure challenge because it has no any right applicant or another staff who can do this staff's job easily. Hence, in labor economy analysis, the firm needs to judge the benefits are much or the losses are much before which decide to dismiss the staff.

What are ethics? Ethics are a set of values or group of moral principles that are right and good a code or principles of behavior or conduct governing an individual or group. For example, when a engineer needs to do any researching jobs which concern to engineering, who needs to increase whose ability as engineer to responsibly confront moral issues raised by technological activity, not always in short term best interest, and long term into decision making ethics are imprecise, complex, and in a given situation may conflict. Who will have these questions to concern before who does his duties, such as does it pass the benefits /harm test? Whom does it harm? Whom does it benefit? Can these be justified, cost/ benefit analysis risk assessment? Does it treat everyone equally? equitable? If not, can the differences be justified? However, any employer needs to concern whose labor ethics issues, who have four aspects need to be considered, such as: On the first concerning aspect, it is working condition ethics, whether the employer's act is moral right when it respects right relevant to a work environment or employment condition of situation. For example, whether the employer can provide whose employees have rights for life, liberty, pursuit of happiness, human rights and non-human rights, e.g. clean and safe working environment or fair salary and welfare, unreasonable normal working hours. On the second concerning aspect, it is duty ethics, whether the employer acts it is right when it conforms with ethics duties to whose employees, e.g. uphold promise, be fair treatment to job nature and duty, respect personal freedom, duty to protect the weak, duty to comply with employment laws, duty to do job to best of ability. On the third concerning aspect, it is utilitarianism ethic, whether the employer has right action consists in producing good consequences to whose employees, e.g. good intentions, outcomes, honesty, fairness, conscientiousness etc. On the final concerning aspect, it is the situational ethics, which means that depending on the specific circumstance, different rights, duties, values, etc. the right circumstance may be applied to whose labors, e.g. whether the workers work in the dirty and dark factory and who need to work abnormal working hours. It seems that if the working environment is not suitable to the employees to feel to work, it will influence the labors raise to work inefficient and poor performance.

So, employers need to concern their ethics to labor, it include moral development to labor, which are often classified such as, obedience or punishment, marketplace morality, conformity, law and order, social contract, universal human rights and integrity whole environment ethic moral development of issues. However, emotion is one important factor to influence labor's individual performance and productivity and efficiency to any employer. How emotional labor and ethic of care will influence productivity. Employers concern care which ought be more than labor itself. Labor's activity that is fundamentally about maintaining, continuing and repairing the working economic world, so that labor can live in it as well as possible. An ethic of labor care is more than a list of moral principles, the ethic of care labor elements, it includes attentiveness, responsibility, competence and responsiveness. However, employers need to make distinctions between " caring for" and "caring about" to labor ethic. "Caring about" is directed toward less concrete objects/subjects. It is a general form of commitment to employees, when "caring for" focuses on a specific object/subject and responds to the particular, physical, spiritual, intellectual and emotional needs of labor. Caring labor is too inclusive of all kinds of economic activities. So employers ought not care relations too narrowly, but should include care is given by extended to employees' families, such as domestic workers and workers in hospitals and teachers etc. service labor occupations. So, labor care ethic relates to the work that employers do under the working conditions within which the employers' labor. Also, a labor care ethic is a deeply relational framework involving both labor care activities and practices as well as a habit of labor care mind. So, employers ought presume that dependent is valued, accepted and universal, it necessitates that care labor to every is shared equally and the society policy also needs to be promoted care labor values to let employers to concern this care labor issue. Care ethic means that empathy and responsiveness, among others, coming out of practices and experiences of " doing care". However, the important aspects of a care ethic that complicates our understanding of the reproduction of alienated labor under capitalism as well as in carrying out care labor, caring for the recipient is an expected part of that work. In labour ethic view, employers ought attempt to answer this question. Does the expectation of such affective emotions necessitate a different formulation of compensation? In examining the relationship between an ethic of care and the alienation under capitalist relations of production. For example: What does make a "good work" ? Is a good worker someone who cares about whose work? How much should the worker care for the recipient of the labour? What does about the customer service representative who care about assisting someone? or does the retail salesperson care about helping someone look good? or does the carpenter care for the wood with which he is working? Whether the worker may or may not take time, be attentive, responsive and responsible. So, I suggest "caring about" and "caring for" the work and the recipient implies a relational experience with others. Many workers care about the outcome of their labour, whether a final product or service. They take pride in their work, they care about doing a good job, they take care of the people with whom who encounter in the process. In this way, workers make their work meaningful, who attempt to connect to it and to those who are "served" when carrying out the work.

Nowadays, human are encountering of an expended service economy, care and the emotional labour involved in such work. For example, luxury hotel workers are interactive service workers both consented to activity investing in the work, also luxury service is not only about what workers do; it is also about how they do it. Luxury service means that how workers make their jobs meaningful, become invested in them, and construct images of themselves as skilled and autonomous. For example, flight attendants who are the caring and emotional labour that is expected of these workers and it is the caring for the recipient, which allows workers to find meaning, creativity and feel connected to the work itself. I also think that labouring makes "real" something outside of the individual, the commodity as value is imposed external to the thing and to the labour itself. Under conditions of private property, the worker is disconnected from whose own creative powers and the objects of the labour become alien to the worker. So, I think employers ought not take away any labour whose individual's specific life, e.g. For long term abnormal working hours will reduce any labour's leisure and family private time.

However, I think labour can divide two kinds of physical labour and emotional labour. For example, the a factory worker works from whose own body and so who is a physical labour. Otherwise, a flight attendant works from whose own feelings and so who is a emotional labour. However, for the particular features of service -oriented labour, who needs to take "caring for" someone is central, necessarily alter these survival techniques. In care work, it is the consumers/recipients of care who expect that those who do caring work care about the work who do and care for the recipients of their care labour, e.g. hotel employees need to shoe genuine care and concern for guests' needs. So, care is the expected and central element of the labour and I think that health attendants and nurses home health carers etc. service workers who need provide more emotional service to whose clients, so who belong to emotional service labour seriously. For example, nursing profession, nurses are thought about as caring, moral creatures who show kindness and comfort to their patients. It is the doctors who are assumed to possess skills and knowledge. How care labour may be negatively affected, such as underpaid, overworked may happen in a situation where the care-giver is compensated unjustly and treated unfairly. Is it possible to argue that if care labour or any labour carried out in the context of a care ethic, the work that is done could be so much better for the whole of society and for the person doing the work and recipients of the work? In an ethic of care that predominates, would we simply value the labour of chid-care workers or home care attendants etc. workers? Would we reflect better compensation, better treatment and better working conditions because our relationship with ourselves and each other are acknowledged and values? Hence, care activities are needed to focus on caring labour, e.g. nurses, personal attendants or home care workers and child care workers. That is, assuming the existence of a care ethic, such questions must be applied to any and all work activities that we do. Does every economic activity contain caring practices, even traditionally non care labour?

I think caring about what we do and how we do it, we may help to improve our relations with others, thus reflecting an ethic of care. Does caring labour help to make invisible, reduce its harm to the self and society? It may be true that workers cared for their work, product or service, this would serve the needs of the employers quite well. How do we care for/about something but against the exploitation produced by capital labour relations? Is it good for society as a whole to care about what you do, care for the work you do, Does the product you make or the service you provide even if it enriches the owner and exploits the worker? What about the office cleaner who cleans the office effectively and efficiently in order to keep whose job that who desperately needs. Should the office cleaner care about doing a good job, care for the faceless people who doesn't know?

A care ethic both encourages this type of work ethic and at the same time, these relations are created and who serve are expected to care for and about the recipients of care, the customer is always right. However, structural inequalities between consumers and workers are normalized in the process. For the nurses and home care workers, the work becomes their own, who become attached to the work, connected to the process and the final outcome, and the work gives meaning to their live. At the same time, when workers don't care about whose work, when they don't care for their charges, or for the service who are offering. Should it, when may the labour be a child care provider neglecting the needs of the child? Or of the overworked social worker dismissing the needs of whose client in order to fill paperwork that who is directed to complete. Hence, I recommend employers need to concern about care is needed such as a practice, value, ethic activity to their labours. The elements of care, its affective emotional and relational qualities help to give meaning to the work for the worker. At the same time, it could be an ethic of care, where individuals view themselves as relational, identifying our connections to others and mutual responsibilities for each other become the necessary conditions for a working class politics.

Labour market equilibrium is a important issue to be concerned in law economy and ethic aspect. Workers prefer to work when the wage is high, and firms prefer to hire when the wage is low generally. Labour market equilibrium "balance out" the conflicting desires of workers and firms and determines the wage and employment observed in the labour market. If labour markets are competitive and if firms and workers are free to enter and leave; the equilibrium allocation of workers to firms is efficient; the sorting of workers and firms are accumulated by trading each other. In fact, labour markets are efficient plays a role by the public policy. Many government programs are often debated whether the particular policy leads to a more efficient allocation of resources or whether the efficiency costs are substantial. Labour market equilibrium occurs when labour supply equals labour demand, generating the competitive wage(w) and employment (E). The wage (w) is the market clearing wage because any other wage level would create either upward or downward pressures on the wage. It would be too many jobs to supply, but the few available workers or too many workers competing for the few available job determined. Due to the competitive wage level is determined in this industry fashion, each firm in the industry hires workers up to the point where the value of marginal product of labour equals the competitive wage. Then, it seems the industry worker's wage level has arrived the maximum labour market wage level. So, employers ought not need to increase whose wage to attract more workers to choose to do whose industry often because it is not reasonable wage level increasing when the labour supply number is enough at the moment. Also the labour market of the industry has implied it's worker demand numbers has arrived the equal level of job supply numbers in the stage. What is caused to happen by worker surplus? When the difference between what the worker receives, that is the competitive wage(w) and the value of the worker's time outside the labour market gives the gains to workers. So, it will cause the excess workers have a value of marginal product that is less than their value of time. In effect, those workers are not being efficiently used by the labour market. So, firms ought to learn how to allocate the right number of persons to different positions that maximizes the total gains and firms ought need to learn how to form trade in the labour market in any efficient allocation way.

Search of labour economy, the central aim is to examine how a work perspective, countries can develop their skills base to increase both the quantity and the productivity of labour employed in the country. Inadequate education and skills of labour development can influence any countries' overall economic development in long term. So, governments need to achieve good policies to solve this issue. Due to skills and education development is central to improve productivity. Because productivity is an important source of improved living standards and growth. Other critical factors include macroeconomic policies maximize opportunities for poor employment growth, an enabling environment is for enterprise development and fundamental investments in education, health and physical to income level households. So, effective skills development systems which is needed to connect education to technical training, technical training to labour market entry and labour market entry to workplace to long life learning to concentrate on providing to low income level households.

Productivity growth can reduce production costs and increase returns on investments. Some of which provide greater income for business owners which some are given higher wages to labours. However, the productivity of individuals may be reflected in employment rates, wage rates, stability of employment, job satisfaction or employability across jobs or industries. The productivity of enterprises, in addition to output per worker may measure in terms of market share and export performance. The benefits to societies from higher individual and enterprise productivity may be evident in increased competitiveness and employment or in a shift of employment from low to higher productivity sector. So, employers can use this method to measure every employee's morality and job behaviour performance to judge whether their job ethic and job attitude whether which can adopt to continue to work in whose organizational environment. If the employer discovered the employee's morality and job behaviour performance and job attitude is not achieved to whose work performance standard, then who can decide to either reduce whose salary or dismiss him/her or not increasing whose salary for long term any decision. So, labour ethic issue is very important to influence economic growth to any countries.

Whether labour ethic has close relationship to economic growth. I feel this issues concerns any stage of the labour life cycle and organization life cycles, it includes the link between the design of economic theory and labour individual morality and job behaviour and performance. In fact, we need to suppose all research questions and labour economy is as mapping to particular stages of an individual's life cycle to labour economy ought be related to the accumulation of human (labour) capital, labour market entry and labour supply choices, behaviour within firms and household decision making. Prior years some researchers had been carrying on observing experiments to the women and men labour work and in whose nature environment for weeks, and then used various treatments, including manipulating the environment in such a way to increase and decrease rest periods. They got result long time working hours and not rest time, it will reduce labours(workers) of productivity. So, it implies the overall productivity and individual productivity will be reduced. Although, the employers have enough workers to work in the natural working environment at the same time, but due to who have no enough rest time to provide to them, then their workers' working performance and efficiency will be fallen. Nowadays, industrialized countries had began to consider how to plan similar welfare reforms, researching the economic reasons and consequences to labour economic issue, such as United States, the United King, Sweden and Germany, it seems economic growth and law ethic has close relationship. However, labour economy includes how to measure labour's emotion to raise productivity, as well as how technological change, education, employment and wages which can assist labour to raise productivity. Due to good labour emotion and labour ethic can raise productivity, then raising productivity can also raise economic growth finally. So, I believe which have close cause and effect relationship.

However, many economists have long been pessimistic that an experimental approach could offer such illustrations of labour ethic and economic growth of cause and effect relationship in their field. Who feel labour bad emotion or bad labour ethic has no any influence to economic growth. In fact, the economic world is extremely complicated, so human needs to have economic laws is set by controlled experiment to measure or judge whether labour ethic and economic growth which has or has no any close relationship. If economists have no such test, economic laws, who can't perform such as the controlled experiments of chemists or biologists very well because who can't easily control other important factors to observe why labour emotion or ethic has reason to influence overall economic growth to any country if they neglect to carry on researching experiment between the relationship of ethic and productivity and economic growth. So I recommend economists need have participants in the natural field experiment to carry on researching to any labour emotion or ethic issue to gather statistic information of population to get prediction more accurately if who want to measure whether labour emotion or ethic and productivity which has close relationship to any country's economic growth for long term.

Why employers need to concern ethic to decide whether outsourcing can raise productivity

Generally, outsourcing can be defined as an organization is entering into a contract with another organization to operate and manage one or more of its business processes. Due to employers face increasing competitive pressure to remain focused, flexible, cost competitive and competent, so outsourcing can access to low cost specialized talent. However, outsourcing means the contracting out of a employer's non core, non efficient, non revenue producing activities to specialists. It is a strategic management tool, such as restructure or contracting out to third party to carry out certain functions efficiently. The most common types of outsourcing are manufacturing outsourcing, information technology outsourcing and business process outsourcing (including processes related to accounting, human resources, benefits, payroll and finance etc. aspects). In fact, employers decide outsourcing reasons which include such as: market pressure to be price competitive, availability of cheap labour elsewhere, abundance of highly talented skilled labour in themselves country, pressure is from investing to cut cost, increase profit and show growth, focusing on core business operations and expanding global presence etc. factors. Many employers begin to concern the ethical and moral implication of outsourcing issue to cause the political and business discussion nowadays. Also, many economists have for-or-against social debates for outsourcing ethic issue. However, outsourcing can bring these benefits to some businesses. For example, if a car can be made more cheaper in China, it should be; if a telephone enquiry can be processed more cheaper in any Asia country, it should be. All such transactions raise real incomes on both sides as resources are advantageously redeployed, with added investment and growth in the exporting country, and lower prices in the importing country.

However, conservative economists argue that the sole mission of a corporation is to maximize profit for the benefits of shareholders. They also contend that in a global economy, outsourcing does not mean net job loss. They argue that more jobs will be created global since the cost labour lowered. The term "global" comes to mind when discussing today's large Corporations. It is hard to say which locally a company belongs to. In fact, outsourcing can also cause disadvantages. Sudden loss of jobs and loss of income can lead to economic depression in smaller regions. As the biggest employer in a those towns/cities closes down factories and start manufacturing in Asia or outsource the manufacturing altogether to a foreign this party. So, the country will raise unemployment rate suddenly when local jobs are outsourced to overseas.

Morality of local employees in favor of outsourcing hiring low wage employees elsewhere is another point of contention of this debate. The (capitalist) economy based on the law of supply and demand. In such economy, allocation or resources, including capital and labour is generally determined by market forces. Therefore, it is reasonable and expectable that companies would seek the best option available to employ their capital and recruit in a global economy. Due to it is assumed that local responsibility has less meaning when the economy and company operate globally. So, it causes any country employers don't concern labour ethic issue after outsourcing influences to its local labour. Nowadays, many employers would agree that the acts of downsizing/outsourcing for pure financial reasons (i.e. choosing short-term investor gain over employee welfare) are very often morally wrong. However, without clear morally relevant distinction (either in academia or business press) between a company's priority to the shareholder and that to its workers, it is very hard defend that position. This is justified because shareholders have taken a risk in placing their money in the hands of the corporation, and are thereby due compensation. Shareholders can potentially lose something who have placed into the corporation. However, workers have placed something at risk when accepting a job, they lose future potential earnings due to corporate outsourcing. At the very least, the worker has foregone other possible job opportunities. Even more importantly, many workers have invested in their houses, their local communities and in their lifestyle with the expectation of a steady income. When the worker's investment in a corporation is not of the same sort as the shareholder's, it constitutes a risk nevertheless, and so the worker's position is not different to that of the shareholder. However, I believe that evaluating the differences of that risk will depend upon of each individual's relationship with the company and their personal values. For example, CEO pay is a completely separate issue on its own. It is a very popular subject in current academic and business press. Even if it is different subject, it has moral implications in regards to outsourcing. In general, CEO can earn a more percent raise to compare to regular worker's percent raise. In common, companies show the reason of CEO percent raise more is that there is enough causation to conclude that outsourcing contributes to profitability / stock price increase of a company, this the rise in CEO compensation. The ethic issue here is that, if the market rewards a company for improving it is bottom line or for cutting costs why is it ethically wrong for a company to outsource at the expense of local labour force. After all, the reason for an existence of company is to provide value to its shareholders. However, I think CEOs aims to achieve themselves benefits, who may improve their bottom line when hurting workers and communities. The morality of further rewarding CEO's who knowingly undertook layoffs of his employees in favor of outsourcing their work to a third party or move those jobs to a low wage country is very troubling.

In fact, outsourcing raises many concerns for working professional for and communities. It has long held personal and community values, such as , loyalty and commitment to employees. However, as much as economic prosperity global trade can bring, if does bring devastation as well. Availability of cheap products is appreciable, but you need to have a job and a income to consume those products. For many, outsourcing hurts at the heart of their livelihoods. Also, I argue to against outsourcing is that growing concern of issues of privacy related to outsourcing information creates an ethical and legal issue. The concern is against outsourcing (in specific cases of Accounting, Human Resource and Medical outsourcing) because of the fear of sensitive information's safety and confidentiality. So, employers ought check references and transcripts and perform background checks to minimize the risk of hiring someone who lacks ethic or morality to do whose outsourcing job duties. Moreover, outsourcing firms may indicate that all of their employees are highly educated, trained professionals of the highest honesty. Finally, I recommend employers ought to consider these questions before who decide to outsource, such as: does stockholders welfare out weight that of a company's employees? Is profit maximization ethical? Is it ethical to reward the upper management for cutting cost by eliminating jobs? Should the compensation for upper management with held if the profit is achieved by outsourcing? Is it ethical to reward a management that repeatedly shown disregard to its employees? (increasing workload, constant layoff, choosing the cheapest labour over quality). Is it right for the public to expect a company to keep all its employment locally, (at a higher cost) but at the same time sell products at comparable rate with foreign companies who use cheap labour? Does a company ethically bound a provide maximum occupation in its home country? Does it have a duty to its local community? In case of outsourcing is the employer ethically bound to retrain the employees? So, all these questions are very important concerning outsourcing influence, if every employer can concern these questions, then who can decide whose outsourcing reason is right or wrong more clearly. To conclude, any employer ought need to decide whether outsourcing is the best of one method to raise productivity for long term strategic plan.

How labour morality can reduce poverty in society

In conclusion, I shall use labour morality can assist society to reduce poverty. In labour economy view, a livelihood comprises the capabilities of assets (including both material and social resources) and activities required for a means of living. A livelihood is sustainable when it can cope with and recover from shocks, maintain or enhance its capabilities and asset, when not undermining the natural resource base. It has three elements: livelihood resources, livelihood strategies and institutional processes and organizational structures. So, I think that productivity will raise, even poverty and crime will be also reduced, due to the low income level householder family which can be upgraded to increase whose income level and quality of living standard to the middle income level householder family. When governments can promote the labour morality to which employers to let them to know labour morality and productivity has close relationship.

How to understand the complex and differentiated process through which livelihoods are constructed, governments need to analyse which countries themselves local citizen to let their knowledge, perceptions and interests be heard. There are three insights into poverty. The first is the realization that when economic growth may be essential for poverty reduction, there is not an automatic an automatic relationship between the two since if all depends on the capabilities of the poor to take advantage of expanding economic opportunities. Secondly, there is the realization that poverty as conceived by the poor themselves. It is not just a question of low income, but also includes other factors, such as bad health, illiteracy, lack of social services etc. Finally, it is now often know their situation and need best and must therefore be involved in the design of policies and project intended to better their lot. So, governments and employers need to identify those issues of subjects areas for effective poverty reduction, either at the local level or at the policy level. This is in principle on open-ended process, certain emphasis is given to the introduction of improved technologies as well as social and economic investments to every country's government. The three fundamental attributes to any developing countries or developed countries themselves countries if which plan to raise economic growth and to reduce poverty to upgrade or low income level householders to rise to the middle income level householder family. The three attributes include the possession of human capabilities, such as education, skills, health, psychological orientation; access to tangible and intangible assets and the existence of economic activities. However, a livelihood comprises the capabilities, assets, including both material and social resources and activities required for a means of living. A livelihood is sustainable when it can cope with and recover from stresses and shocks and maintain or enhance its capabilities and assets both now and in the future. To solve poverty problem, it includes not only physical and natural resources, but also every country's social and human capital issues. Every country's government also needs to facilitate an understanding of the causes of poverty by focusing on the variety of factors at different levels that directly or indirectly determine or constrain low income level householder's access to and assets of different kinds. Also every country's government needs to assess the direct and indirect effects on low income level householder's living conditions then, for example one dimensional productivity or income criteria.

Over the various components of a livelihood, the most complex is the portfolio of assets out of which people construct their living. This portfolio includes tangible assets, such as stores, e.g. food stocks, stores of value, such as gold, jewelry, cash saving and resources, e.g. land, water, trees, live stocks farm, equipment as well as intangible assets, such as claims, for example, demands and appeals which can be made be material, moral or other practical support and access, which is the opportunity to practice to use a resource, store or service or to obtain information, material, technology, employment, food or income. Hence, if employers can provide enough capital input to make whose labours feel fairness, satisfactory and reasonable working environment and compensation. I believe that these satisfactory demand of labours who can raise productivity to their employers more easily. In labour economic view, any employers, governments or companies organizational resources inputs can divide four kinds of capital nature. Firstly, the natural capital is natural resources stocks, e.g. soil, water, air, genetic resources etc. and environmental services, e.g. hydrological cycle, pollution sinks, etc. from which resources flows and services useful for livelihoods are derived . Secondly, economic or financial capital is the capital base, e.g. cash , credit/debt, savings and other economic assets, including basic infrastructure and production equipment and technologies which are essential for the pursuit of and livelihood strategy. Thirdly, human capital is the skill, knowledge, ability to labour and good health and physical capability important for the successful pursuit of different livelihood strategies and finally, social capital is the social resources, e.g. networks, social claims, social relations, which people draw when pursuit different livelihood strategies, requiring co-ordinated action. So, any country or employee which has a plan to know how to allocate which resources efficiently, it will raise productivity and economic growth and poverty reducing more easily. So, it seems labour morality can raise productivity which has close relationship to any employer, even labour morality and economic growth which has close relationship to any country. So, any country and any employer which ought not neglect labour morality for long term.

Raising consumers' consumption desire

CHAPTER FOUR

WHAT IS THE RELATIONSHIP BETWEEN BEHAVIORAL ECONOMICS AND PSYCHOLOGY

At the core of behavioral economics is used psychology of economics analysis to improve economics on its own terms generating theoretical insights, making better prediction of field consumption of behavioral phenomena, and suggesting better policy to any company or government decision makers. It rejects economic theories based on utility maximization, equilibrium and efficiency. It is useful because it provides economists with a theoretical framework that can be applied to almost any form of economic (and even non-economic) behavior to predict behavioral consumption more easily to businessmen. So, behavioral economy is different to general economy concept, it applies psychological methods to attempt to predict consumption behavior.

Simpifying much assumption that are not central to the economic theory to apply to psychological behavior. Other assumption simply acknowledge human limits on computational power and self-interest. These assumptions can be considered procedurally rational because human needs to solve problems that are often so complex that who can't be solved exactly by even modern computer technology. So, if businessmen apply psychological method to predict behavioral consumption to earn the more benefits or profit, it is more reasonable to compare to apply computer methods to predict consumption behavior.

Theories in behavioral economics should be judged by reality, generality and tractability concepts to apply why we (consumers) do our behavior (consumption of choices) from psychological analysis. We share the positivist view that the ultimate test of a theory is the accuracy of its predictions. But we also believe that better predictions are likely to result from theories with more realistic assumptions. In psychology, such as connectionist models that capture some of the essential features of neural functioning, which are based on utility maximization, yet are reaching the point where they are able to predict many judgemental and behavioral phenomena. Contrary to the positivistic view, however, businessmen ought believe that predictions of consumers' feelings (e.g., of subjective well-being) should be an important goal to earn more profit more easily.

Most of the ideas in behavioral economics are not new. When economics first became identified as a distinct field of study, psychology didn't exist as a discipline to apply to economy subject. For example, "invisible hand" and "the wealth of Nations" which belong to theory to moral sentiments, which laid out psychological principles of individual behavior that are arguably as profound as whose economic observations. Another example, such as a simple model of social utility means that one (consumer) or person's utility was affected by another person's , such as whose family or friends' influence why to choose to buy this product or use this service in consumption market.

Nowadays, economists hoped their discipline could be like a natural science to apply psychological methods to predict behavioral consumption to assist businessmen to earn more economic benefit or to reduce cost or profit to win whose competitors. But psychology was not very scientific. However, later economists are very much appealed to psychological insights to attempt to assist businessmen how to predict consumers how who will prefer to choose to consume to buy this product or use this service.

Throughout the second half of the century, many criticisms of the positivistic perspective took place in both economics and psychology. The economists of the time had less disagreement with psychology than they realized. They assume without foundation that behavior always aims at the goal of maximum pleasure and minimum pain; but behavior is not goal-oriented. Also the economists of the time believed false conclusions are drawn from false psychological assumptions to predict consumer individual behavioral consumption wrongly.

The importance of psychological measures and bounds on rationality. These commentators attracted attention, but did not alter the fundamental direction of economics. One development was the rapid acceptance by economists of the expected utility and discounted utility models which are making decision under uncertainty and choice, respectively. Whereas the assumptions and implications of utility analysis are rather flexible, and the expected utility and discounted utility models have numerous precise and testable implications. So, it seems economy and psychology can have close relationship to be connect to be applied to predict consumer individual consumption of behavior to assist any enterprises can earn more profit or more economic benefit more easily in global competitive consumption market nowadays.

In behavioral economy view, economists began to accept counter examples that could be not be permanently ignored, developments in psychology identified promising directions for new theory to be applied how to assist businessmen to predict behavioral consumption to earn economic benefits or profits. Beginning around 1960 year, psychology became to be dominated by the brain as an information-processing device replacing the behaviorist conception of the brain as a stimulus-response machine. The information-processing permitted a fresh study of neglected topics like memory, problem solving and decision making. These new topics were more obviously relevant to the conception of utility maximization than behaviorism had appeared to be to apply how to predict behavioral consumption in traditional psychological method.

However, behavioral economy and psychological consumption prediction method, psychologists began to use economic models as a benchmark against which to constrast their psychological models. Early research in behavioral consumption methds have followed these steps. First, identify assumption or models that are used by economists, who expected utility and discounted utility. Second, the assumption or model is a rule out alternative explanations (such as subjects' confusion or transactions costs). And third, the assumption or model creates alternative theories that generalize existing models. The final is to construct economic models of behavior using the behavioral assumptions to test them from the third step. This final step of economic models of behavior has only been taken more recently to be applied to predict why the consumer prefers to choose to do this behavioral consumption of decision finally.

What is the standard economic model? It is the standard economic model, the way most economists think about consumer welfare and consumer choice. What is the rationality in the standard economic model? The standard economic model relies heavily on the assumption that consumers are rational. Standard economic model assumes that consumers are fully aware of all the options who have, who can always and consistently , rank whose options in accordance with their preferences, and always choose the option, who like the best option. Thus, what the assumptions of the standard economic model of consumer are? The assumptions include consumers act with full information, consumers have known preferences, consumers choose the best option available. In economic view point, It concerns consumers will compare cost to make decision to choose to buy which kind of product which can satisfy whose needs among of similar products of comparision.

The standard economic model of consumer behavioral prediction method advantages includes: A logically consistent theory of consumer behavior can be built, that theory can be used to make predictions about consumer behavior and those predictions can be compared with reality and those models often correspond to actual behavior of consumption reasons. What is the inconvenient truth? It includes clear evidence from psychology has shown that the rationality assumptions of standard economic model are wrong. Evidence from psychology has shown that consumers often are irrational and also who are predictably irrational. So these are wrong view point to influence how economists judge what cause consumption of behavior. Thus, it beings this question? What is mean of predictably irrational? It means that of irrational consumers were irrational in random ways, who would cancel each other out, leaving the overall outcomes determined by the behavioral consumption of rational consumers. As that case, behavioral economic theories that ignored irrational behavioral consumption would work just fine. But, psychology has shown that consumers are irrational in similar and predictable ways. Therefore, irrationality doesn't cancel out and can't be ignored to judge why the behavioral consumption has been caused.

How can behavioral economists judge each behavioral consumption cause? Economists will see evidence that consumers often are unable to make use of what consumers know about whose available options and whose preferences to figure out the best available option. However, although economic theory doesn't always assume self-interested behavior to any consumers, as a practical matter, most applications of economic theory assume that consumers act according to self- interest to decide every behavioral consumption of choice. For insurance industry is one good behavioral economy market example, insurance market competition can make rational consumption. Such as competitive market in auto vehicle accident insurance will charge very high rates to some insurance buyers who might to drive a fast speed, but unsafe motorbike, this one might argue will protect the driving insurance buyers from taking stupid risk. So learning can make rational consumers. Even if consumers are predictably irrational, who can learn from their families and other consumer' or friends behavioral mistakes, therefore, over time irrational consumers will learn to be rational to make the most irrational consumption. As a result, there are few opportunities to learn from consumer individual mistakes of any consumption of decision. Finally, if there are many potential; bad choices and one good consumption of choice, it might take a lot of costly experimentation to figure out the right consumption of choice. Thus, the standard economic model of behavioral consumption of prediction method, which is standard economic theories assume that consumers are rational, strong-willed , and self-interested, but evidence from psychology shows that who are not and that evidence also shows that consumer individual irrationality has predictable features. So, it seems behavioral economic model can make economic predictions more accurate by using the evidence on consumer individual predictable irrational behavioral prediction in any kind of the similar products in competitive market nowadays.

CHAPTER FIVE

HOW TO APPLY PSYCHOLOGICAL METHOD TO PREDICT CONSUMPTION OF BEHAVIORS

The methods to predict how to cause the (consumer's)person's consumption of behavior are the same as those in other areas of economic and psychological methods. In fact, behavioral economics relied heavily on evidence generated to predict behavioral consumption by experiments. More recently, however, behavioral economists have moved beyond experimentation and the full range of methods are employed by economists. The experiments played a large role in the initial phase of behavioral economics because experimental control is exceptionally helpful for distinguishing behavioral explanations from standard ones.

Suppose we observed this phenomenon in these any one of cares, in the form of failures of legal cases to settle before trial, costly divorce proceedings, and labor strikes. They are phenomenons of human' behaviours are caused by costs and benefits measurement of result. It implies the married people or the legal compensatory amount or labor strikes compensatory benefits will evaluate whether thier economic benefit is more or loss is more to decide divorce behavior or legal trial behavior or labour strikes compensatory behavior . So, consumer individual psychological behavior and economic benefits has close relationship to cause how consumer who prefers to make any consumption of choice every day. As the failures of legal cases to settle before trial , the behavioural economy concept would be difficult to tell whether rejection of offers was the result of reputation-building in repeated games, agency problems (between clients and lawyers) confusion why the lawyer' client (appellant) who choose to continue to attempt to pay legal fee to find the lawyer to appellate the case if the case is fail at the first time . However, in these game experiments of failures of legal cases to settle before trial, costly divorce proceedings, and labor strikes. These explanations are ruled out because the experiments are played once, have no agents, and are simple enough to rule out confusion. Thus, the experimental data clearly establish that subjects are expressing concern for fairness.

Other experiments have been useful for testing whether judgment errors which individuals commonly make in psychology experiments also affect prices and quantities in markets, such as shareholder's individual investment behavior. The lab is especially useful for these studies because individual and market-level data can be observed. Although behavioral economists relied on experimental datato predict shareholder's individual investment behavior, however, behavioral economics subject is seen as a very different method from experimental economics. As noted, behavioral economists are methodological profession. They define themselves, not on the basis of the research methods that who employ, but rather their application of psychological insights to economics.

Experimental economists, on the other hand, define themselves on the basis of use of experimentation which is as a research tool. Also, economists have made a major investment in developing experimental methods that are suitable for addressing economic issues, and have achieving among themselves on a number of important issues. For example, experimental economists often make instructions and software available for precise replication, and raw data are typically shared for reanalysis. Experimental economists also insist on paying performance-based. However, experimental economists have also developed rules that many behavioral economists are likely to find excessively . For example, experimental economists rarely collect data like demographics, self-reports, reponse times and other cognitive measure which behavioral economists have found useful. Descriptions of the experimental environment are usually abstract rather than which are carried on experiment in the outside world because economic theory rarely makes a prediction about how a happen would matter, and experimenters are concerned about losing control over incentives if choosing strategies with certain labels is appealing because of the labels themselves. Finally, economic experiments also typically use "stationary replication", in which the same task is repeated over and over in each period. Data from the last few periods of the experiment are typically used to draw conclusions about equilibrium behavior outside the lab. When economists believe that examining behavior after it is of great interest, it is also obvious that many important aspects of economic consumption of individual behavior to every individual consumer. The consumer's individual consumption of behavioral choose is like the first few periods of an experiment rather than the psychological methods to predict behavioral consumption.

Supposing if we need to make decision of marriage, educational decisions, and saving for retirement, or the purchase of large durables like houses, sailboats, can cars, which happen just a few times in a person's life, a focus on behavior is clearly not warranted. All said, the focus on psychological realism and economic applicability of research promoted by the behavioral-economics perspective suggests the usefullness research outside the lab and of a broader range of approaches to laboratory research. So, economists realize that who have ideal opportunity to learn by trial-and-error, in a stationary environment, and uses the opportunity to learn how to carry on experimenting any psychology and behavioral researches in lab experiment environment.

What is psychology of consumption behavior?

Psychology is the science of human behavior and mental consumption processes. In consumption process behavior, it is any consumption behaviors as well as consumer mental consumption process is consumer individual internal experiences, comparison with alternative products, products choice of the best, making decision to consume or not consume for the product. So, advertisers often persuade to influence consumers' behavior to attract them to choose to buy whose products.

Why businessmen need to learn consumer psychology? Because psychology can help businessmen scientifically to evaluate common consumer beliefs and misconceptions about consumption behavior and consumption decision making mental processes. Consumption scientific psychology has four basic goals: To describe , explain, predict and change consumption behavior and consumption decision making mental process. Consumption psychological information is based on evidence, this is information based on direct observation and measurements with consumption behavior with scientific method. How are typical images of psychology? Consumption psychologists need to use scientific method to help businessmen to think what predicts who own, make a list of words would who use to describe a psychological scientist and what use to describe a psychological scientist and what images the businessmen have. However, consumption psychologists have difference ways of looking at the same problem for the businessmen, which is why there are so many sub-fields of consumption psychology. Consumption psychology's roots began in philosophy, but the focus changes to a scientific focus consumer.

Behaviorism is focused on consumer buying behavior that can be measured and observable. This returned the scientific approach to consumption psychology. Consumption behaviorist's believe consumers are controlled by their environment. Consumption behaviorism focuses on consumption observable behavior. However, consumption cognitive psychology believes that consumption behaviors are preformed because of the product ideas and thoughts. The cognitive perspective focuses on such consumer decision making and choice processes, such as perception, memory and thinking to the product.

The two categories of consumer's behavioral consumption of decision

The field of consumer's behavioral consumption of decision research, on which behavioral economics has drawn more than any other subfield of psychology, typically classifies research into two categories: judgement and choice. Judgement research deals with the processes people use to estimate probabilities. Choice deals with the processes people use to select among actions, considering of any relevant judgements who may have made. Everyday, we, such as consumers need to make probable judements. Due to judging the likelihood of events is central to economic life. For example: Will you lose your job in a poor economic environment? Will you be able to find another house you like as much as the one you must bid for right away? Will the government raise interest rates in this year or next year? Will a merger strategy increase profits? These questions are answered by some process of judging likelihood. The standard principles used in economic to model probability judgement in economic are concepts of statistical sampling, which are concerned probabilities in the face of new evidence. However, it requires a separation between previously judged probabilities and evaluations of new evidence. However, (consumers) people often overestimate the probability who previously attached to events which later happened. This leads to "secondguessing". For example, Monday morning quarterbacking and may be partly responsible for lawsuits against stockbrokers who lost money for their clients. (The clients think the brokers should have known). For example, anybody has tried to learn from a computer distance learning manual has seen the classroom learning of knowledge in action. Another example for making probability judgements is called "representativeness": People judge conditional probabilities like P(hypothesis /data) or P(example/class) by how well the data represents the hypothesis or the example represents the class. Representativeness is an economical shortcut that delivers reasonable judgements with minimal effort in many cases. For example, in judging whether a certain student (University customer) described in a profile is, say, a psychology major or computer science major, the student decides how well the profile matches the psychology or computer science career to the student generally. So, University can read the student profile to predict whether the student will choose to study psychology subject more prefer or computer subject more prefer to predict whose computer or psychology student numbers more accurate in the year.

Many studies show how this sort of feature-matching can lead people to underweigh the "base rate", in this example, the overall frequency of the two majors. Another byproduct of representativeness is the "law of small numbers": Small samples are though to represent the properties of the statistical process that generated them (as if the law of large numbers, which guarantees that a large sample of independent draws does represent the process, is in a hurry to work). Field and experimental studies with basketball shooting and betting on games that people believe that there is positive attitude that players experience the "hot hand", when there is no evidence that such an effect exists.

For example, how the government tax department can judge whether the company's financial report has not been misled from accounting auditor's moral behavior, how to predict consumer's brand choice behavior and how to control students' learning behavior in classroom . It is important to judge whether it is either a good attitude or bad attitude from the consumer's personal behavior in the past. A consumer's good attitude to the product or the service consumption provides good consumption experience, close to optimal, answers when time or capabilities are limited, but it also needs logical principles and leads to situations. So, optimal is largely a critique (a reasonable one) of the later applied research. Otherwise, a consumer's bad attidude to the product or the service consumption provide poor consumption experience to buy the product or use the service again. Thus, the consumer's good or bad past buying experience to the product or to use the service will have help to assist the businessman how to predict whose consumption behavior next time.

Assume that people misspecify a set of hypotheses, or encode new evidence incorrectly. For example, assuming that people believe hypothesis A is more likely than B will never encode pro-A evidence mistakenly, but will sometimes encode pro-B evidence as being supportive. For another example, investors will think there is wide variation in skill of, say, mutual-fund managers, even if there is no variation at all. (A manager who does well several years is a surprise if performance is mistakenly thought due to nonreplacement, so concluding that the manager must be really good.) A question concerns stock market, such as: Overreacts in the long term. In their model, earnings follow a random walk but investors believe, mistakenly, that earnings have positive attitude. After one or two periods of good earnings, the stock market can not be confident that exists and hence expects, but since earnings are really a random walk, the stock market is too pessimistic and is underreacting to good earnings news. After a good earnings, however, the stock market believes many investors are increasing. Since, it is not the stock market is too optimistic and overreact. So, investor's past experience to earn or loss from the share, which will influence whose invetment behavior to choose to buy the share next time.

For another example, valuable consumer products (A $100 wireless keyboard, a fancy computer mouse, bottles of wine, and a box of chocolate) are sold to postgraduate (MBA) business students. The students were presented with a product and asked whether who would buy it for a price equal to the last two digits of their own social security number (a roughly random identification number required to obtain work in the United States) converted into a dollar figure, e.g. , if the last digits were 99, then the postgraduate business students will accept the hypothetical price was $99 to buy any of it for a price to the last two digits of their own social security number . After giving a yes/no response to the question. Would you pay $99? subjects were asked to state the most who would pay (using a procedure that gives people an incentive to say what who really would pay). Although subjects were reminded that the social security number is essentially random, those with high numbers were willing to pay more for the products. However, many studies have also shown that the method used to elicit preferences can have dramatic consequences.

Nevertheless, when required to make an economic decisions-to-choose a brand of toothpaste, a car, a job, or how to invest, people do make some kind of decision. Behavioral economists refer to the process by which people make choices with ill defined preferences as "constructing preferences". So, psychologic methods can be used to predict why the consumer choose to buy the product as well as any consumer seems who needs to evaluate whether who will earn more benefit or low to choose to buy the brand of product or use the service to achieve the best benefits. However, in classical consumer theory, preferences among different commodities are assumed to be invariant with respect to an individual's current consumption. Specifically, people seem to dislike losing commodities from their consumption much more than they like gaining other commodities. For example, the research of "contingent valuation" studies that attempt to establish the dollar value of products which are not routinely trades. Contingent valuation is often used to do government cost-benefit analysis or establish legal penalties from environment damage. These surveys typically show very large differences between buying prices (e.g. paying to clean up oil of beaches) and selling prices (e.g. having to be paid to allow beaches to be ruined) to reduce environmental pollution from the low cost method for government spending.

Nowadays, there are many USA manufacturers use behavioral economy methods to predict consumer individual behavior, a quarter of the wealth in the USA has more interesting opportunities to do behavioral economies. They find that motivated sellers should regard the price who paid as a sunk cost and choose at a nominal loss from the purchase price. Sellers' listing prices and subsequent selling behavior reflects to nominal losses. There are some cases in which no effect would be expected, such as when products , such as house or antique dealers' products are purchased for resale rather than for utilization. For example, Do art or antique dealers like with pieces who buy to resell? What about surrogate mothers who agree to bear a child for a price paid in advance? Reference points can also serve as social focal points for house or antique products or surrogate mothers whose behavioral judging performance.

For an interesting example from corporate finance. In general, when managers whose firms face possible losses (or declines from a previous year's earnings) are very reluctant to report small losses. As a result, the distribution of actual losses and gains show a very large at zero, and hardly any small reported losses (compared to the number of small gains). A manager who does not have the skill to shift accounting profits to erase a potential loss (i.e. has some earnings in his pocket.) is considered a poor manager. It seems that the bad performance manager whose behavior is bad to mislead public to believe his firm have better performance in this year. Hence, in the mental accounting view, people(accountants) set up mental accounts for outcomes which are psychologically separate, much as financial accountants lump expenses and revenues into separated accounts to guide managerial attention. Otherwise, mental accounting stands in opposition to the standard view in economics that it predicts, accurately , that people will spend money coming from different sources in different ways. So, a generalization of the notion of mental accounting (the accountant's mislead financial report performance) , which aims to let investors and consumers have more confidence to choose to invest or to choose to buy it's products or consume its service more easily. So, it explains why the accountant needs to mislead to report it's earns are more than loss in every year.

BEHAVIORAL ECONOMY CONCEPT

Prospect theory

What is preferences ove risky to behavioral consumption. Such as prospect theory is experimental choices more accurately than (EU) because it gets the psychological of judgement and choice right. It consists of two main components, a probability weighting function, and a "value function" which replaces the utility function of (EU) to any consumer when who needs to choose to buy any product or consume any service by more than one choice. The weighting function P(P) combines two elements: (1) The level of probability weight is a way of expressing risk and (2) Captures how sensitive people are to differences in probabilities. New information of any products can help any decision maker to feel better to make better final purchase decisions. These theories effect may explain demand for information in settings like medicine or personal finance, where new information usually does not change choice, but relieves anxiety people have from knowing there is something who could know to choose to buy the medicine or borrowing loan of low interest payment. So, new information of any products can reduce consumer individual risk to choose to buy.

However, the planning problem for economic agents who would like to behave in fashion and discussed the important time discounting for choice. Most big decisions, e.g. savings, educational investments, labor supply, health and diet, crime and drug etc. decisions use have costs and benefits which occur at different point in time. Thus, time discounting is basically standard time discounting plus an immediacy effect, a decision discounts delays in equally at all moments except the current one, caring differently about well being. This functional form provides one sample and powerful model of the taste to individual to make right or reasonable behavior economic decision. However, most analyses of choice assume that people integrate new consumption with planned consumption. It is infeasible and perhaps for this reason, descriptively inaccurate. When people make decisions about new sequences of payments or consumption, they tend to evaluate them in isolation, e.g. treating negative outcomes as losses, rather than as reductions to their existing money flows or consumption plans.

How to decide fairness and social preferences. The assumption that people maximize their own wealth and other personal material goals just self-interest is a correct simplification that is often useful in economics. However, people may sometimes choose to spend their wealth to punish others who have harmed them, reward whose, so who have helped, or to make outcomes more fair. Just as understanding demand for products requires specific utility function. So. on economic view point, utility function concept can influence consumer choice. if the consumer feels the product has more utility, then who will prerfer to choose to buy the product. Otherwise, if who feels the product has less utility, then who will not perfer to choose to buy the product.

Behavioral economy can also use to assist firms to choose right behavior to decide to do any matters. I show hypothesis to establish any reference level of consumer surplus and product profit. Both sides are entitled to any firm's levels of profit, so price changes which threaten any matter are considered unfair. So raising any product price, it will reduce consumer surplus and is considered unfair. But the cost of a firm's inputs rises, subjects said it was fair to raise prices. Because not raising prices would reduce the firm's profit (compared to the reference profit). Everyday observation that firms don't change prices and wages as frequently commonly.

For example, when the fourth hary potter story book was released in summer 2000 year, most stores were allocated a small number of books that were pre-sold in advance. Why not raise prices or auction the books off? It is possible that it concerned about customer goodwill and excess demand to cause book stores limit such book price increases. Offended consumers are often able to affect firm behavior by media attention or provoking legislation. For example, scalping tickets for popular sports and entertainment events (resulting them at a large premium over the printed ticket price) is constrained by law in most countries. For example, some countries have "anti-laws" penalizing sellers who take advantage of shortages of water, fuel and other necessities by raising prices after natural disasters. So, the countries' governments can protect which citizen benefits to balance the natural resource supply and demand to sell in the reasonable price fairly after the natural disaster occurrence. This is utility function concept. Because the book store believes the fourth hary potter story book will be excess demand and reader goodwill is good. So the books' utility function is enough to prepare to sell to readers, which do not need to raise price to attract readers to read. Also, scalping tickets for popular sports and entertainment events will rise ticket price to be limited level because the popular sports and entertainment players believe who have attrative ability to attract full ticket buyers and whose numbers will exceed seats demand. So, the ticket numbers utility are enough and which are not need to raise ticket price too much. Also, shortages of water, fuel and other necessities by raising prices after natural disasters, because government make whose citizen has limit number of water, fuel and other necessities supply to keep enough utility function to satisfy whose needs. So, the nature resources do not need to raise price when natural disaster occurs.

A few years ago, responding to public anger at rising CEO salaries when the economy was being restructured through downsizing and many workers lost their jobs. Otherwise, some countries passed a law prohibiting firms from deducting CEO salaries for tax purposes beyonded $1 million a year. However, because some countries need to earn much tax income from these high salary CEO income every year. So, these countries do not suggest to pass a law to probibit firm from deducting CEO salaries for tax purpose. So, utility function can be applied to company benefit. If the company hopes to limit the CEO salary, then it will limit whose CEO 's duty (reducing utility funtion to whose duty). Aim to avoid to pay more salary expenditure to the CEO , when the country's economy is poor and it believes there are less consumers prefer to consume more. Otherwise, if the company does not hope to limit the CEO salary, then it will not limit whose CEO'duty (increasing utility function to whose duty). Aim to hope who can help whose company to earn more profit, when the country's economy is good and it believe there are many consumers prefer to consume. On the other side, if the country tax department hopes to earn more salary tax income, it will choose not to pass a law prohibiting firms from deducting CEO salaries for tax purposes beyonded $1 million a year. In the behavioral economy concept, the government tax department hopes to earn more salary tax when the economy environment is not good or it is worse to compare last year's economy environment. Thus, behavioral economy concept will be applied to company profit intention or country income intention or individual consumption intention.

Behavioral game theory

How can behavioral game theory apply to company income intention ? Behavioral game theory has rapidly become an important foundation for many areas of micro economic theory to any organizations, such as bargaining in decentralized markets, outsource contracting and organizational structure. The descriptive accuracy of game theory in these application can be questioned because equilibrium predictions often assume strategic reasoning and direct field tests are difficult to any organizations. In fact, behavioral game theory uses any experimental evidence and psychological research to generalize the standard assumptions of game theory to any organizations how which choose to make profit intention.

One component of behavioral game theory is a theory of social preferences for allocations of money to oneself and others. Another component is a theory of how people choose in one shot games or in the first period of a repeated game. For example, in share buying and selling market, shareholders shall buy or sell shares from their judgement in the economic cycle market everyday. So share investment is seemed as allocation of game to these shareholders. Also, shareholders whose mind can influence whose psychological behavior to decide how to invest whose shares in their share investment economic activities. The component of behavioral game theory can include a model of learning to either individual or a population. Also, game theory is one area of economy in which serious attention has been paid to the process by which can equilibrium comes about. Many learning theories have been proposed and carefully tested with experimental data. Theories about population never predict as well as theories of individual learning through who are useful for other purposes. So, behavioral game theory can be applied to these complex environments. e.g. consumer supermarket purchase, share market etc. for these business organizations research.

How to apply behavioral game theory to macroeconomics and saving aspect? Many concepts in macroeconomic probably have a behavioral style that could be influenced by research in psychology. For example, it is common to assume that prices and wages are in nominal terms, which has important implications for macroeconomic behavoir. Behavioral economics suggests some ideas for among consumers and workers, perhaps it is influenced by workers' concern for fairness.

An important model in macroeconomics is the life cycle model of savings or permanent income hypothesis. This theory assumes that people make a guess about their lifetime earnings profile, and plan their lifetime earnings profile, and plan their savings and consumption in each period has diminishing marginal utility; and preferences for consumptions streams are time-separable (i.e. overall utility is the sum of the discounted utility of consumption in each separate period). The theory also assumes people lump together different types income when they guess how much money who will have (i.e. different sources of wealth are different). So, why many young people won't spend too much money for unnecessary expenditure, e.g. entertainment easily. Because who plan to save for their old age to use in their long time life time.

A behavioral life cycle theory of savings in which different sources of income are kept track of in different mental accounts. Mental accounts can reflect natural perceptual or cogitive divisions. For example, it is possible to add up the travellers' paycheck and dollar value of whose frequent flyer miles, but it is simply unnatural to do so. It is important to note that many key implications of the life-cycle hypothesis have never been well supported ,e.g. consumption is far more closely related to current income than it should be according to theory. However, predictions can be improved by introducing utility functions with habit formation in which utility in a current depends on the reference point of previous consumption, and by more carefully accounting for uncertaining about future income.

For example, in the accountancy (economic) professional view point mental accounting is only one of several behavioral approaches that may prove useful. Economics is money illusion, it is the tendency to make decisions based on nominal quantities rather than converting those figures into real terms by adjusting for inflation. Money illusion seems to be pervasive in some domains. So, it appears that employees don't seem to mind if their real wage falls as long as their nominal wages doesn't fall.

How can behavioral game theory apply to company income intention? Labor macroeconomics is involuntary unemployment. Why can some people not find work beyond of switching jobs, or a natural rate of unemployment?

A popular account of unemployment pushs that wages are deliberately paid above the market clearly level, which creates an excess supply of workers and hence unemployment. But why are wages too high ?
As efficiency wage theory shows that paying workers more than who deserve is necessary to ensure that who have something to lose if they are unemployed, which motivates them to work hand and economizes on monitoring.

How Another viewpoint indicates that employer and worker is such as into a gift exchange relationship. Employers pay more than who have to as a gift and workers repay the gift by working harder than necessary. They show how gift exchange can be an equilibrium and show some of its macroeconomic implications. In labor economics, gift exchange is clearly evident of experimental labor markets. In practical working environment, firms offer wages; workers who take the jobs than choose a level of effort, which is costly to the workers and valuable to the firms.

For example, firms and workers can enforce wages, but not effort levels. Since workers and firms are matched for just one period, and do not learn each other's identities, there is no way for either side to build reputations or for firms to punish workers who chose low effort. However, self interested workers should shirk, and firms should anticipate that and pay a low wage. In fact, firms deliberately pay high wages as gifts and workers choose higher effort levels when they take higher wage jobs. It seems that it has strong relationship between wages and effort is stable over time.

For another example, standard life-cycle theory assumes that if people can borrow, they should prefer wage profiles which maximize the present value of lifetime wages. Holding total wage payments constant, and assuming a positive real rate of interest, present value maximization implies that workers should prefer declining wage profiles over increasing ones. However, in fact, most wages profiles are clearly rising over time which is such as a phenomenon. Rather, workers derive utility from positive changes in consumption, but have self-control problems.

If any company has any good wages profiles would prevent them from positive changes in consumption, but have self-control problems that would prevent them from saving for later consumption of wages were more front-loaded in the life cycle. In addition, workers seem to derive positive utility from increasing wage profiles, it is perhaps because rising wages are a source of self-esteem and the desire for increasing payments is much weaker for non wage income. The standard life-cycle of labor supply also implies that workers should substitute labor and leisure based on the wage rate who face and the value who place on leisure at different points in time. If wage fluctuations are temporary workers should work long hours when wages are high and short hours when wages are low. However, because changes in wages are often persisting and because work hours are generally fixed in the short-run. So, it is difficult to tell whether workers are substituting. So, if the company can have good method to decide when to rise salary or wage level , even reduce salary or wage level, as well as how much rising or reducing salary or wage level is the suitable in different time. If the wage fluctations are reasonable in the most suitable time, the labor turnover numbers will not be reduced easily.

How can behavioral game theory apply to individual business income intention? For example, taxi drivers who target daily will drive longer hours on low income days and will drive less hours early on high income days. This behavior is exactly the opposite of substitution. Also inexperienced taxi drivers support the daily targeting prediction. But experienced taxi drivers don't have negative elasiticies, either because target minded drivers earn less and self select or taxi drivers learn over time to substitute rather than target. Perhaps the simplest prediction of labor economics is that the supply of labor should be upward sloping in response to a increase in wage. Suppose to the inexperienced taxi drivers will attempt to drive long hours if who can feel or predict the taxi passengers number will reduce on the low income day. Otherwise, the experienced taxi drivers will attempt to drive less hours if who can feel or predict when the taxi passengers number will increase on the high income day. So, these experienced or inexperienced taxi drivers whose decison of driving long hours or less hours is depended on whose feeling of taxi passengers number who is high or low.

How, behavioral game theory applys to investor behavior. In finance, standard equilibrium models of asset pricing assume that investors only care about asset risks if who affect marginal publicly available information to forecast stock returns as accurately as possible the efficient markets hypothesis. When those hypotheses do make some accurate predictions and some investors in assets have limited rationality of behavioral finance. Also, in share stock market, it is common, shareholders should not want to trade with them, but the volume of stock market transaction is large. So, it presents data on individual trading behavior which suggests that the extremely high volume may be driven, in part, by overconfidence on the part of investors. Thus, if the company's share numbers buying and selling transactions are very large in the year. Then, it will influence many investors have more confidence to be encouraged to choose to buy the firm's shares in the year. Otherwise, if the company's share numbers buying and selling transactions are less in the year. Then, it will also influence many investors have less confidence to be encouragd to choose to buy its' shares in the year.

For another example, behavioral game theory applys to property agent's behavior. Property agent's individual behavior is similar to share agent's individual behavior. In the economy view point , property agent bases a list price for a house on the selling prices of nearly houses that is similar ("comparables"). Every nearest neighbour techniques bases on similarity is also used in credit scoring and other kinds of evaluations. Also, one firm whose every share sale on the selling price is comparable to its similar firms whose every share price in its same business industry. The shareholder will evaluate whose every share issued sale price in the stock (share) market. Otherwise, in behavioral economy view, for example, property or share buyer who has risky choice to decide to buy in the property or share market. It is a process of comparing the similarity of the probabilities and outcomes in two gambles and choosing on dimensions which are dissimilar.

As we mentioned above, behavioral economics simply includes an interest in psychology. In fact, we believe that many familiar economic distinctions do have a lot of behavioral content, they are implicitly behavioral, and could surely benefit from more explicit ties to psychological ideas and data. However, some people do not feel psychology and economy which have close relationship. Such as, substantial debate is ongoing in psychology about whether knowing the precise details of how the brain carries out computations is necessary to understand functions and mechanisms of driving car skill at higher levels, (knowing the mechanical details of how a car works may not be necessary to turn the key and drive it). So, the drivers who concerns more safe to their families and themselves, who will prefer to pay more money to buy the more safe vehicle to driver. Otherwise, the drivers who disconcern safe and concern money save, who will choose to pay less money to buy the less safe vehicle to drive.

Behavioral game theory can apply to price behavioral elasticity for how firm's price decision. For example , it is the distinction between short run and long run price elasticity which concerns behavioral economy. In fact, economy needs have theories concepts to support any evidence to prove any matter has happened. Concerning short run and long run price elasticity cause and effort issue, with a casual suggestion that the run is the time it takes for markets to adjust, or for consumers to learn new prices, after a demand or supply stock. Adjustment costs undoubtedly have technical and social component, but probably also have some behavioral factors influence in the form of gradual adaption to loss and learning. So, if there are many consumers who believe the product is reliable to use and the brand is famous, the product's price won't be push down often and it has less price elastic. Otherwise, if there are many consumers who do not believe the product is reliable to use and the brand is not famous, the product's price will be push doen often and it has more price elactic tendency.

Another macroeconomic model which can be interpreted as implicitly behavior is that business cycles can emerge if it is not general price inflation, so why the consumers shall not decide to buy this kind of product in the competitive market. So price when the market price inflation, consumers will not choose to prefer to spend to buy more food to eat or products to use. Otherwise, when the market price is stable, consumers will choose to prerfer to spend to buy more food to eat products to use. So, inflation will influence consumption of behavior.

Behavioral economic simply includes an interest in psychology. In fact, we believe that many familiar economic distinctions do have a lot of behavioral content, they are implicitly behavioral and could surely benefit from more explicit ties to psychological ideas and data. However, some people do not feel psychology and economy which have close relationship. Such as psychology is about whether knowing the precise details of how the brain carries out computations is necessary to understand functions and mechanisms at higher levels. (knowing the mechanical details of how a car works may not necessary to turn the key and drive it.)

Most psychology experiments use indirect measures like response times, error rates, self reports and natural experiments due to brain has been fairly successful in codifying what we know about thinking. However, pessimists think brain scan studies won't add much. The optimists think the new tools will lead to some discoveries and the potential is great that they cannot be ignored. However, economy needs have theories or concepts to support evidence to prove why any matters had happened. An example, is the distinction between short term and long term price elasticity. This distinction, mentions between of them, with a casual suggestion that long run is the time it takes for markets to adjust, or for consumers to learn new prices, after a demand or supply shock. Adjustment costs undoubtedly have technical and social components, but probably also have some behavioral factors influence in the form of gradual adaption to loss and learning.

However behavioral economy theory can be applied to organizational behavior, organizational behavioral theory concerns that organizatonal contracting are shot through with implicitly behavioral economics. Some economists motivate the incompleteness of contracts as a consequence of rationality in foreseeing the future, but do not tie the research directly to work on memory and imagination. For example, agency theory begins with the presumption that there is some activity the agent doesn't like to do. Why markets are better at making dramatic changes than managers influence cost. So, influence costs are the costs managers preform for projects who like or personally benefit from like promotion or raises. A lot of influence costs are undoubtedly inflated by optimistic, each division manager really does think their division desperately needs funds and social comparison of pay and benefits. Otherwise, why are salaries kept so secret? In all these cases, conventional economic behavior has deeper psychological questions of where adjustment costs, effort and influence costs come from. So, it beings these questions: Could these phenomena surely produce surprising testable prediction? Is psychology regularity an assumption or a conclusion?

Behavioral economics generally begins with assumption rooted in psychological regularity and asks what follows from those assumptions. An alternative approach is to work backward, regarding a psychological regularity as a conclusion that must be proved an explanation that must be derived from deeper assumption before we fully understand and accept it. The alternative approach is caused by a fashionable new direction in economic theory and psychology too, which is to explain human behavior as the product of evolution. However, we may not believe that behavior of intelligent, modern people lived in socialization and cultural influence can only be understood by guessing what their lives were like and how their brains might have adapted generally. There are other models that treat psychological regularity as a conclusion to be proved rather than an assumption to be used. Such models usually begin with an observed regularity. However, I think economic factor can influence consumers to make who feel the more reasonable psychological decision to make the more right behavior. Thus, economy and psychology has close relationship to influence consumer individual decision.

Economists have for deriving behavior from first principles and rationalizing apparent irrationality. Theories of this sort are useful behavioral economics and what fresh predictions do they make. However, critics have pointed out that behavioral economics is not a unified theory, but is instead a collection of tools and ideas. This is true. However, some economists believe that economic models do not derive much predictive power from the single tool of utility maximization. The goal of behavioral economic is to develop better tools that, in some cases, can do both jobs at once.

Economists like to point out the natural division of labor between scientific disciplines: Psychologists should concern to individual minds, and economists to behavior in games, markets, and economies. But the division of labor is only efficient if there is effective coordinaton, and all too often economists fail to conduct intellectual trade with those who have a comparative advantage in understanding individual human behavior. The only question is whether the implicit psychology in economics is good psychology or bad psychology. We think it is simply unwise, and inefficient to do economics without paying some attention to good psychology.

Can predict consumer behavior with web search?

In behavioral economy view point, it can be applied to predict why consumers buy products from internet. Recent work has demonstrated that web search volume can "predict the present", meaning that can be used to accurately track outcomes, such as unemployment levels, auto and home sales and disease prevalence in near real time. Consumers are searching what for online can also predict their collective future behavior days or even weeks in advance. For example, specifically businessmen can use search query volume to forecast the opening weekend box-office revenue for feature films, first month sales of video games and the rank of songs, finding in all case that search counts are highly predictive of future outcomes from online google research. Finally, businessmen can reexamine previous work on tracking trends and show that, perhaps surprisingly, the utility of search data relative to a simple auto regressive model is modest.

Nowadays, people increasingly use the internet for news, information and research purposes. From this perspective, it is a short step to conclude that what people are researching for today is predictive of what who will do in the near future. For example, consumers may search to prepare to buy a new camera, moviegoers may search to determine the opening date of a new film, or to locate cinemas showing it and individuals planning a vacation may search from a places of interest, to find airline tickets, or to price hotel rooms. So online can aggregately count of search queries related to retail activity. Movie going or travel might be able to predict collective behavior of economic, cultural, or political interest. Determining the nature of behavior that can be predicted using search, the accuracy of such predictions and the time scale over which predictions can be usefully made are therefore all questions of interest.

Researchers have focused on the observation that search " predicts the present". For example, Ettredge et al (2005) found that counts of the top 300 search terms during 2001 to 2003 year were correlated with US Bureau Of Labor statistics Unemployment Figures; Cooper (2005) et al found that search activity for specific cameras during 2001 to 2003 year correlated with their estimated incidence and Eysenbach (2006) found a high correlation between clicks on sponsored search results of flu-related keywords and epidemiolopical data from the 2004 to 2005 year Canadian flu season.

Thus, motivated , I indicate one example how investigates whether search activity is a systematic leading indicator of consumer activity by forecasting. For first example, supposing to opening weekend Box-office revenue for 119 feature films released in the united States between Oct. 2008 year and Sept. 2009. For second example, supposing to first month sales of video games across all gaming platforms, e.g. Xbox, Play station etc.) for 106 games released between Sept. 2008 and Sept. 2009 year. These search data can be collected from yahoo using research rank from the current and previous weeks.

Can online search also predict the near future? A finding that may apply usually to a wide range of consumer behaviors , e.g. airline travel, hotel vacancy rates and auto sales and economic indicators , e.g. real-estate prices, credit card and confidence indicators. It seems all research based predictions simply models to build on publicly available information. For movies, baseline predictions can be used a linear model that includes production budgets, the number of screens on which each movie opened and box office projections from the Hollywood Stock Exchange (HSX) (hsx.com) on online, play money prediction market that is known to generate information prediction. For video games, many of the key indicators of revenue, including production budgets and initial available. Thus, it seems that businessmen can attempt to use internet (online) search technological method to search past information to concern whether what number of customers will be estimated.

Can firm's conduct and behavior factor influence consumption of behavior ?

In behavioral economy view point, it can explain how firm conduct and behavior factor can infuence consumption of behavior. The usual assumption about the objectives of firms made by economists is that firms seek to maximize profit. The means that firms feel that who are protected against the possibility of new entrants, and proceed to maximize short-run profits. Firms feel that the barriers against new entrants ensure that their profits won't induce new firms to enter the industry and to reduce competitors enter to industry to raise consumers' choices to buy any similar products.

A major challenges to the profit maximization objective has come from proponents of the view that modern larger corporation are under a managerial control, which it is argued leads to the pursuit of other objectives, such as growth. The pursuit of non-profit objective is not unique to managerial-controlled firms, although the growth of such firms and of theories about than have emphasized these types of objectives.

Another view has focused on the controllers of the firm, whether owners or managers, having a wider range of objectives and that the achievement of profit maximization and the cost minimization requires considerable time and effort by the controllers. Thus, the controllers have incentives to forge profit maximization, unless who are forced to do so. Under oligopoly, firms can earn profits above the normal level, e.g. one country has only two electricity power companies are existing in the country's energy supply market. They may change a profit maximizing price, but actual reported profits may be less than potential profit.

This could raise from technical inefficiency or from higher than necessary payments to the factors of production. The technical inefficiency can arise since it takes effort by the controllers to reach full efficiency and which may be willing to make necessary effort. The higher payments can involve higher salaries to the controllers of the firm. For either reasons, company needs to concern how to report profit fall below true profit of the firm, with the difference used to finance inefficiency and higher factor payments in fair business conduct behavior. Particularly, company also need to concern how to carrying on fair business conduct behavior, e.g. none mislead advertising information, correct profit differentiation financial information, product reputations of the existing products presentation, none mislead consumption motives performance (which favor the established over the unestablished) and lower trade-in values of second –hand products of entrants (particularly in the car market). So, it seems that any one firm none mislead conduct behavior factor can influence consumer choices to increase or decrease to buy the firm's products in fair buying and selling transaction.

Another view point, for same products differentiation none mislead conduct factor is also important to influence each consumer behavior. For example, cars don't have a common prototype and each manufacturer must design its particular model. In constant , for a product like sugar , there is a common prototype, and differentiation through branding is within the discretion of the firm involved. This for some good product differentiation may be benefit whereas, for other products differentiation depends upon the activities of the firms involved, although the costs and benefits to the existing firms varies between profits. However, the height of the barrier to entry by product differentiation is likely to be influenced by the conduct and behavior of the firms involved, and thus in the case , there is an element of firm's behavior and conduct can influence any consumer buying behavior of choice to its products.

How to apply behavioral economic principles to assist policy makers or decision makers to make more reasonable decision.

Behavioral economics theories can also apply to assist any policy makers to make right and reasonable decision in right time. I shall indicate new principles to recommend and I also shall give any psychological cases to explain how policy makers can apply behavioral economic theories to judge how to make their any decision is the most right and the most reasonable.

Behavioral economy is an independent and demonstrates real economic well-being. It aims to improve quality of life by promoting innovative solutions that challenge mainstream thinking on economic, environment and social issues. Also, behavioral economy is different branches of more alternative economies into a form that is useful primarily for policy-makers. I think behavioral economy can be given an aid to policy makers how who use economic tools to the broader policy making community by providing a theoretical behaviour for many policy approaches to be used.

The standard economic analysis assumes that humans are rational and behave in a way to maximize their individual self-interest. This rational man assumption indicates a powerful tool for analysis. However, it has many shortfalls that can lead to unrealistic economic analysis and policy-making. Also, I think behavioral economics and psychology has these principles to influence human behaviour. These principles include, such as below:

In common, people do many things by observing others and copying; people are encouraged to continue to do things when they feel other people approve of their behaviour. People do many things without consciously thinking about time. These habits are hard to change. There are cases where money is de-motivating as it undermines people's intrinsic motivation. People want their actions and commitments to be values usually. People put undue weight on recent events and who can't calculate probabilities well and worry too much about unlikely events and who are strongly influences by how the problem/information is presented to them. People need to feel effective to make a change, even just giving who the incentives and information is not necessarily enough in any environment usually. So any policy maker ought concern about what the acceptable degree is when who choose to decide to make any new policy in whose country. If who can predict whether whether whose country's citizen will or won't accept whose new policy implement and know why some won't accept whose new policy implement and why some accept whose new policy implement, then who can decide to do any economic activities more reasonable, e.g. investment to build public hospital or public school in the location; spending this expenditure to education or medical more.

In fact, much of our behaviour is strongly influenced by other people's behaviour. Social learning is a process by which we take in the behavior of others to learn how to behave. In more complex situations with which we are unfamiliar, we consciously watch and learn from the behavior of others. For example, when use a new library for the first time. When we make a conscious decision on how to behave, our sense of social identity is important, we think: how would other from my group behave in this situation? So, the policy marker will need to make to compare the economic benefits to choose to build either library or public school between of them to satisfy readers need or students need more in the location.

In situations where there is high social capital. i.e. where there are strong networks between people and a high level of mutual trust, so its seems other people's behaviour and our sense of social identity may be extremely important in influencing our own behavior and policy makers ought need to know how to judge their behaviour whether their behavior is either right and reasonable or wrong and unreasonable in any learning process of environment. The standard economic theory is tried to explain where people's preferences come from, so it does not take account of the direct influence of the people's behaviour and social norms on our behaviour. The theory assumes we independently know what we want and that our preferences are fixed. This standard theory is very good at explaining short-term decision making for policy makers only. In decision marker view point, for example, I want green vegetables and choose fruits as they are on special offer in short term, but it cannot explain longer term changes in preferences. Now, I only choose organic food for long term because orgnic food can have more clean and no pollution to compare general green vegetables and fruit. Thus, the learning process environment will influence the food consumers who prefer to choose to buy organic food more than general green food in supermarket.

For driving example, it would require too much effort to look up all the rules when driving in a new country, to find out all the fines/punishments for failing to meet the rules, to work out the probability of being caught and the possible costs, before deciding how to drive there. Instead we just copy other people, and perhaps adjust our behaviour according to the feedback we receive. However, some psychologists indicate to see people how to behave, especially in crises situations and when others are experts. These psychologists have identified that we are open to influence from people in authority or people we like. When we are influenced by authority, an expert, someone with legitimate power to direct our actions, someone who can either reward or punish us. The effects are less likely to be lasting than we are influenced by someone we like. Thus, learning process of environment can influence any person's psychological behavior change easily. However, some people's psychological behaviour is similar to economic behaviour to judge to make any decision. For example, why do you wear a seatbelt in your car? Most of us wear seatbelts as it has became normal behaviour, everyone does it. We neither evaluate the likelihood of having an accident, nor the chance of getting caught without our seatbelt on and incurring a fine. The enforcement of seatbelt wearing is now hardly necessary, as it has become a social norm.

What does this mean for policy makers? Policy makers focusing only on economic analysis may often devise a system that has an immediate effect. In psychologists view this issue point, knowing that there is a fine for speeding and a high likelihood of getting caught, the driver will probably drive more slowly, but who will drive just as fast one who realise the chance of being caught is low. However, of policy makers can change the social norm, perhaps in this case by encouraging us to frown on others who drive dangerously fast with campaigns against dangerous driving, then less enforcement will be needed after the change. In other words policy makers might want to take preferences as fixed in the short term, but they should consider shifting preferences in the medium term.

An example where policy appears to have successfully changes people's preferences in the US and Singapre and Hong Kong is banning smoking in public places. This change appears to reduce the social proof of the amount people smoke in private places and public places both also. It seems that government policies can influence the decreasing numbers of consumers require to buy cigeratte to smoke habitually, due to fine and punishment is regulated to be ban effectively. Such daily routines quickly became habits. Even when we consciously think about what we do, it can be difficult to change our behaviour. Perhaps I think it is a good idea for people to use public transport, but I do not know where the bus stop is or when the bus runs. I think to use private car to drive to work place is more preference choice. The reward feeling , my journey by car was easy and free to reinforce my old bad habit. Psychologists theories on changing habits generally involve raising it to a conscious level where we can consider the merits of alternative behaviour.

In our learning process in environment, this is followed by adopting the new behaviour, which, with time, becomes frozen as a new habit. Thus, I think that we need have regulation to control my behaviour, then we can change my behaviour to be new habit from old habit of behaviour easily, such as consumption behavior. For example, human blood sale is an economic product, due to paying donors for blood would increase supply. Supplies would be provided at a cost advantage in the future, if demand continued to rise. Such as supplies to hospitals for blood will has cost from donors when there are many patients need much blood to use to treat any diseases in any hospitals. Otherwise, if there are not many patients need much blood to use, but there are many donors have effort to provide blood to any hospitals, then it will be economic inefficiency and it is highly wasteful of blood. Thus, the hospitals need to predict when there are many patients need much blood or there are less patients need less much. Then, hospitals can pay cheap cost to donors for blood supply. Thus, the learning processing for donors for blood supply is needed for hospitals.

For shareholder behavioual learing process in share investment environment example, if you hold some shares in a firm that has gone down in value. What do you do? Many people hold on to their shares in this situation, in the hope that they will recoup their losses. Conversely, when shares have gone up in share, people are happy to sell them to realise their gain, A similar behaviour is also observed for professional traders who tend to hold on to shares with a loss for longer than those with a gain. The traders who exhibit this type of loss to a lesser degree tend to be the more successful ones.

For another learning process environement example, this is a case where the theory is directly applicable within economic cost-benefit-type analyses that include valuations of no-market products, such as valuations of pollution damage. Policy makers have a choice as to whether-to-accept, and as these may vary by up to a factor, the outcome of such an analysis many well depend on which value is chosen. When a policy maker reasonably has a right to something that might be taken away from them, the willing-to-accept value would be used. On the other hand, when the policy maker only reasonable has a right to the status quo and an improvement is proposed, then the willingness-to-pay is the correct value to use. Thus, for valuations of pollution damage, policy makers need to learn whether pollution damage cost is higher or pollution bringing benefit is higher to make reducing pollution decision for long term. In generaly, people are expected to rationally make the best choices given their preferences, independent of how these choices are presented. Therefore more information and choice is always considered good. Using this theory, policy makers should ensure that people always have as much information and as many things to choose between as possible, the process of introducing policy is irrelevant. Thus, gathering information can assist policy makers to choose right decision for pollution damage benefit or cost behvioral choice to their society for economic benefit.

So, a participatory approach not only improves policy, it also makes to any policy makers more happier. In most cases these principles cannot be used directly as part of any mathematical economics analysis, but highlight situations where this standard analysis will not accurately describe human behaviour and therefore might have unintended consequences when implemented in policy. However, that the policy implications could be quite powerful as the behavioural approach provides quite different lines of analysis to the standard economic model. It is heartening to see policy makers focusing more on the psychology of behaviour when devising policy. So behavioral economics is a relatively new field of economics that attempts to incorporate insights from psychology into economic models and analyses. As above cases seem any policy maker's economic activities which are relative to whose psychology's decision.

However, psychologists are often interest in understanding at the level of individual or social group of behaviour, the primary interest in economic is usually in understanding how behaviour and interactions play out in a system to shape economic outcomes. Economists are interested in system-level outcomes, such as the level and path of wages, the effect of taxes on economic output, how rates of savings respond to interest rates etc. However, those economic outcomes depend on complex interactions of individuals. So, behavioural economy concerns to how to judge individual to do the reasonable or right behaviour to hope to get the reasonable economic result as well as it's goal rather to help improve any policy makers to understand their behaviour in ways that allow economists to make better predictions and suggest better economic policies. However, new elements about information processing or individual preferences might impact economic models and analyses in any learning process environment.

Is psychology influencing all field of economics? It is possible that behavioral economy needs theoretical contributions and laboratory evidence to support to make any reasonable or right decision to any policy makers. This type of work generally uses existing observational data and estimates relationships between variables of interest by either using naturally occurring variation in the data i.e. natural experiment.

Perhaps more than any other field, behavioral economics has had a large impact on finance to the point that behavior finance is often considered a separate field as opposed to being of behavioral economics. Also, public economic is the study of how government policies in fluence economic markets. A primary emphasis of public economic involves the topic of taxation. Otherwise, the biggest impact that the behavioral approach has had in economic is the analysis of retirement saving to influence any employees' decisions about their retirement savings. However, when employees can do make any active savings choices to prepare their retirement. If employers can assist whose employees to design any methods to allocate fund, then accumuates interest and is tax free until the retirement funds are withdrawn to every retirement employee. The tax advantage make effort to save for retirement.

Behavioral economic is in understanding how individuals do or do not smooth consumption over time. Smoothing consumption is a standard economic models. It suggests that individuals should borrow or save in order to consume a similar amount throughout one's lifetime. For example, a teacher who is paid a salary 12 months a year, who should not spend all whose salary within one year. Rather, the teacher should smooth whose consumption over the 12 month period. How to allocate to spend paychecks, food and social security payments which concerns the teacher decide to spend whose salary efficiently. Hence, who needs to plan how he shall spend whose one year salary to be reasonable use in the future.

Public economic is to understand how people respond to taxation and social benefit programs. This has been an area that has seen an explosion of behavioral work in recent year. i.e. how taxpayers can experience over-withholding and receive tax refunds from tax department. Policymakers and insurers are also increasingly turning to psychology for approaches to improve health behavior. Traditionally health-policy focused largely on information provision, assuming that as long as individuals were well informed, their decisions would maximize their health choices. For example, influential work on the effects of smoking taxes, however, well being of smokers appears to increase with higher taxes to influence health behaviours are not completely rational.

Behavioral economic has also had a small impact on the study of criminal behaviour. For example, individuals are not less likely to commit a crime when who are 18 age and the pubishment of doing so increases dramatically. However, some economists explain the motivations people have for giving to charity and who understand the psychological motivations for charitable giving. So, it seems that charity award giving has probable to reduce 18 age people who choose to do crime behaviour easily because who feel who have effort to assist charity in their life time.

Industrial organization economists study why firms exist and how which function and compete with each other. Insights and psychology and behavioral economics have made a significant contribution to develop that model the interactions of profit maximizing firms with their customers. In fact, firms often need to evaluate whether their products if prices are needed to set what of price of level is the most reasonable and attractive to customers to choose to buy their products.

For cell phone plan sale example, individuals choose cell phone plans with fixed minute allotments and steep charges for going over the minute limits, but frequently exceed their plan limits. This behavior is the best explained by a model in which people overestimate the precision of their demand forecasts. So, cell phone firms need to research how cell phone plans with fixed minute allotments and steep charges of cell phone call fee charge plan is the most acceptance method to cell phone clients generally. However, cell phone call charge plan and various cell phone product features and the way cell phone clients allocate their limited attention affects cell phone products markets which are external important factors can influence any cell phone clients why who will choose to use the cell phone call plan because any cell phone will be very large durable product to any cell phone consumer after who choose to buy the cell phone product. Hence, who will not often choose to use the old cell phone firm call charge plan if who feel it provides the excellent cell phone call service and reasonable phone call plan to use to compare other cell phone call plans in the cell phone call market.

Hence, the cell phone call firm needs to make marketing research why consumers need to choose to use which cell phone call plan among of other cell phone call plans in the cell phone call market. Also, researching the cell phone buyers' choice behaviour why who choose to buy the cell phone to use issue, which will have influence to the cell phone buyer why who choose to use the cell phone call charge plan because expensive cell phone is needed to use excellent quality of cell phone call service usually. Otherwise, cheap cell phone is needed to use poor quality of cell phone call service usually. So, cell phone call plan is needed to follow the cell phone quality and price to be used and they ought have direct relationship to influence why the cell phone buyer who chooses to use the cell phone call plan.

Finally, behavioral economy can also apply to be used to labor supply as a motivating in negative or positive labor supply elasticities in taxi driving example. For example, it is possible that taxi drivers work fewer hours when wages are high-consistent with a model of daily income targeting. This finding is that when wages are high (perhaps it is raining and thus it is easy to find people who want a taxi ride), taxi drivers are able to hit their daily target quickly and then go home. However, when wages are low, taxi drivers are not able to hit their target quickly and thus work additional hours in order to hit their target. It means taxi driver's behaviour produce the effect that taxi driver works more when wages are low than when wagers are high. This work has resulted to analyze taxi driver of labor supply decisions with daily reference points in non taxi domains. So, instead of the weather and client numbers and taxi charge factors, the factors of taxi drivers' hours worked and the quality of service is produced is another important factor to influence any taxi drivers' numbers to supply to the taxi market.

Behavioral economic has also influenced the understanding of how staffs can impact worker productivity and job satisfaction. For example, it is possible that poor cooperation can cause worker productivity decreases and it can also cause poor job satisfaction to the worker. So, when working environment can impact productivity, social comparisons can have an impact on job satisfaction as well as the worker's job satisfaction and search intentions are affected by knowing about the salaries of their peers in whose firm. Hence, the worker's positive or negative psychological feeling to whose employers which will have effort to influence whose working performance and productivity to whose firm in possible.

Behavioral economic is increasingly being used in the field of development economics or low income countries.

Such as, how Philippines can offer commitment to individuals who wanted to save money in whose country or how Philippines can change to smoking behaviour when commitment devices were offered to Philippine smokers. So, Philippines policy makers need to concern resource scarcity and resource allocation issue to solve how to let its low income level householders can raise to the middle income level to achieve the high income level householders and the low income level householders whose income level is not distant very much.

Analysis whether behavioral economy and psychology which has close relationship.

Finally, I shall analyze whether the relationship between the discipline of behavioral economy and psychology which two branches are totally opposite or if the behavioral theories is only complement that mainstream economics. I think study of economy is the behavior of the complex human beings; this science examines how people choose to act and allocate resources in different market situations. So the economic analysis, is based on the implications that arise from a series of simple assumptions (which are sometimes cited as unrealistic) regarding the human nature. However, in psychological view, the individual is characterized by unlimited rationality and by the ability to follow time consistent, in every situation, his self-interest. In these conditions, behavioral economic attempts to consider a field of analysis in the study of economic phenomena.

Because economics deals with the study of human behaviour on the market, it highlights the human character of the science and the fact that, besides of all the patterns and models, the analysis refers to the real individual. It is also behavioural because it attempts to combine approaches from several sciences mainly from economics and psychology, and also from sociology, philosophy, anthropology or biology. This is not an easy mission, in the conditions in which these various disciplines have adopted in time different approaches that became, in many ways, contradictory. So, behavioural economics is that a multidisciplinary approach will increase the explanatory power of economics.

On one hand, there are specialists two argue that behavioural economic is a field of economics that continues the hand, there are others who see it as a distinctive school of thought, which proposes a new paradigm. However, behavioural economists propose a multidisciplinary study, criticize certain assumptions on which the traditional model is built (such as rationality and self-interest, in their unlimited form), resource to experiments (the classical method of psychology) to validate some assumptions, propose new theories (such as the prospect theory) and advance different interpretations of the economic behaviour, e.g. how to maximize consumers satisfy their needs. This issue is concerned to concern consumption of psychology and social economic situation research aspect.

Also, I think that behavioural economics can help the economic science by describing more realistically the utility functions of the individuals. This field of study is based rather it is a natural extension of the basic approach. However, it is can be claimed that behavioural economics is also built on the premise that psychology methods and assumptions are equally important. Also, models of behavioural economics, allow the utility to depend on the differences between one's own level and a reference level. People are sensitive to changes and preferences are not stable in time. The vision of behavioural economics concerning the inter-temporal choice (which assumes that individuals prefer immediate gains and delay unpleasant activities) seems to be more appropriate to the human behaviour that the one of the traditional model (which assumes that utility is updated over time).

How can consumer debt management psychological factors influence consumption behavior?

In behavioral economy view point, it can be applied to explain why consumer debt management psychological factors can influence consumption behavior. Some consumption psychologists had investigated several psychological variables which have been suggested as causes or effects of debts. Economic and demographic factors can predict debt category well to support this influence of factor. How can consumer manage money skills to pay debt which can influence when who plan to consume? Debtors were more likely to buy cigarettes and Christmas presents for children than non-debtors. Conclusions must be qualified because of low return rates, but the results suggest that a complex of psychological and behavioral variables affect debt and are affected by it. It is argued that these variables are linked to the psychology.

In general, economical environment is poor, it will cause many unemployed people, even some people will loan debt to pay daily essential expenditure from banks. If those debtors can't manage whose debt to be better to spend. Whose behavior will cause who do not have more spending desires often. Because these debtors will feel themselves as being in a community where debt was more common and more tolerated than non-debtors. The whole question of the classification of products a necessities or luxuries and its consequences for purchasing behavior is of current interest in economic psychology. Since debt is associated with poverty and poor people tend to give external reasons for economic phenomena, such as poverty and unemployment, causality may run the other way. In either case, however, there should be a positive correlation between external control and debt. There have different variables offer explanations of debts at different levels. One factor may be a consequence of another, or the mechanism by which it takes effect (for example, different patterns of economic socialization might generate different attitudes towards debt).

Some debtors need to borrow debt (loan) for house purchasing need. So, if the house loan debtors who need to pay back whose house loan to bank for long time. It is possible that their house loan will influence to reduce to spend much of daily consumption behavior to buy non luxury and daily essential products for long time. Thus, the result is these house loan debtors will reduce every day essential expenditure, such as food and soft drink, entertainment etc. to consume too much to compare to non house loan debtors for long time. It seems that retailers can attempt to apply debt management behavior to predict consumer shopping of desires.

In conclusion, I shall indicate two theories to explain why economy and psychology has close relationship to influence human do any behavioural economic activities daily. For example, through the prospect theory, behavioural economics adds new parameters to improve the mathematical modelling method, which was advanced by economists for decisions taken under uncertainty. However, the theory also proposes a slightly different interpretation. The results are interpreted by the individual as positive or negative deviations from a reference point, which has a neutral psychological value. Last but not least, in addressing social preferences, behavioural economics adds parameters that increase the concern of decision-makers to also assess their utility function in relation to others. For another example, the choice theory; secondly there is not a common consensus between the specialists of behavioural economics regarding the variables that should be included; and finally, many variables that affect the behaviour are not quantitative, but qualitative, and cannot be precisely measured. The findings of behavioural economic are relevant and can help the mainstream theory by providing a more realistically base of study. However, this argument has contributed to the development of behavioural economics, because there are a large number of phenomena that cannot be entirely explained by the mainstream economics.

So, why in the beginning, I indicated why behavioural economics does not imply the totally exclusion of the neoclassical approach and the most studies in this area try to provide a more realistic base of the standard theory. In the concluding, I believe that in time, behavioural economic models will replace the simplified ones, based on unlimited rationality. Also, economists have provided a great importance to the quantitative structures, departing from the human nature. However, behavioural economics can become truly revolutionary only it will always be receptive and will provide a critical insight to their own theories and perspectives, and especially the ones regarding the aspects that they reproach to the traditional economic theory. However, I also feel that the individual's behaviour on the market is determined only be economic factors. In brief, individual choices and, by this, the demand variation are explained only and the variations in the prices of products/services and the available personal income. Am important discussion in the field of determine directly the economic behaviour of an individual (like the sociological and psychological of factors) are actually active elements in the process the reshaping of the utility functions. Finally, in my view, I believe that the conduct of the market phenomena, as it occurs in reality. In this sense, the research of behavioural economics aims to see how the neoclassical model could be improved, using mainly psychology concepts. Although, there are some specialists who argue that behavioural economics can be an alternative to the neoclassical theory.

Finally, most findings, of my study conducted in this book, modify some of standard economical assumptions, in order to provide a greater psychological realism. However, the additions proposed by behavioural economists simply recognize the human limitations on (mentally) calculations, will and self-interest. So, I think psychology and economy has close relationship to assist any policy makers or decision makers to do any economic psychology daily. Because the purpose of economics is to better understand and explain the conduct of the economic activities as which occur in reality. Otherwise, human being is complex and its behaviour and constitution is studied by all the social sciences. Consequently, multi and interdisciplinary approaches can bring real benefits to the economic science, by providing a more realist foundation to cause any policy makers or decision makers how to decide to make any behaviours or economic activities by behavioural economic activities support daily.

Can price change influence consumer behavior?

In behavioral economy view point, it can explaine why price change can influence consumer behavior. In general, under short –run profit maximization,

the price was seen as a mark –up marginal cost with the marketing determined by the elasticity of demand. However, economists have used these methods to determination of how prices change behavior. The first is the indicated prices are determined relative to costs by firms in the pursuit of objectives. In the view point, the first is firms are price-makers and let prices in a way which think will achieve these objectives. Subject to constraints arising from demand and cost conditions. The second is theory of perfect competition, firms are effectively price-takers and the interaction between demand and supply in the market set price. So, firms are regarded as price-takers, and hence not in position to set prices, such as price-adjuster . The third is the idea of observing the process of price decision-making and seeking observation is on the prices of price determination. Their view is expressed as price is based on full average cost , including a conventional allowance for profits and full average cost . Is determined as follows? price or direct cost per unit is taken as the base, a percentage addition is made to cover overhead or on cost or indirect cost, and a further conventional addition of percentage is made for profit. This, it seems price change behavior can influence consumer individual consumption behavior to any products.

How can constructive consumer choice processes influence consumption behavior?

Consumer decision making has been an interest in consumption behavior research, e.g. how technological changes, an information explosion factor can influence consumer individual choice decision to buy any products. Due to limited processing capacity, consumers often don't have well-defined existing preferences, but construct them using a variety of strategies contingent on task demands. Rapid technological changes for instance, has led to multitudes of new products and decreased product lifetimes. In addition, new communications media, such as the world wide web have made amounts of information on options potentially available (Alba et al. 1987). It seems time pressure, such as fast product lifetimes and new communications, media, internet advertisement can influence consumers how to make decision to buy any thing which is the best to them, e.g. choice of gathering products of advertisement information to buy products from internet (electronic shopping) instead of traditional visiting shops consumption behavior. So, new information advertisement media, e.g. internet advertisement consumer information media will influence consumer individual decision tasks. For example, a consumer may be fairly certain about the values of some of the attributes to choose to buy which kind of mobile phone from electronic shopping easily at home. However, the consumer may not have information for all of the mobile phone options on some attributes (e.g. reliability information would not be available for a new mobile model) from internet advertisement. In addition, some attributes, such as safety may be difficult for consumer to trade off; making trade off requires possibly accepting a loss on such an attribute with potentially threatening consequences.

What is characteristics of consumer decision strategy in product choice process? It includes the total amount of information processed, the selectivity in information processing, the pattern of process, (whether by alternative brand or by attribute). First, the amount of information processed is very a great deal. For example, a mobile phone choice may involve detailed consideration of much of the information available about each of the available mobile phone, as implied by more rational choice models, or it may have a consideration of a limited set of information (e.g. repeating what are choices last time). Second, different amounts of information can be processed for each attribute or alternative (selective processing), or the same amount of information can be processed for each attribute or alternative (consistent processing). For example, suppose a consumer considers the mobile phones to decide that life time is the most important attribute, processed only that attribute and chooses which mobile brand, with the famous brand value on that mobile phone attribute. Third, choice process would involves on that attribute. This choice process would involve highly selective processing of attribute information (since the amount of information examined differs across attributes), but consistent processing of alternative mobile phone brand information, since one piece of information is considered for each mobile phone. The fact that working memory capacity is limited effectively requires selective attention to information, e.g. internet advertisement media.

In general, the more selective consumers are in processing information, the more susceptible their decisions may be to factors that influence the salience of information, some of which may be irrelevant, such as different mobile phone brands of product life time comparing information. Information may be processed primarily by alternative, in which multiple attributes of a single option are processed before another option is considered, or by attribute, in which the values of several alternatives on a single attribute are examined before information on another attribute is considered. For example, a consumer might engage in attribute processing by examining the price of each of the mobiles, concluding that mobile brand (A) was the most expensive, another mobile brand (B) was the least expensive, and the another mobile brand (C) had a very good price . However, the consumer could process in an alternative-based fashion or is design by examining the reliability, price, safety of mobile phone brand (A) in order to form an overall valuation of that mobile phone brand (A).

Finally, an important distinction among strategies in the degree to which are compensatory. A compensatory strategy is one in which a good value on one attribute can compensate for a poor value on another. A compensatory strategy thus requires explicit trade off among attributes. Deciding how much more one is willing to pay for very good rather than average reliability or long useful life time in a mobile phone involves making an explicit trade -off between reliability long useful life time and price for examples. Thus, in general, constructive consumer choice processes attribute , such as the product's price, quality, life of time , reliability, design , brand information of media sources as well as electronic internet shopping or visiting shopping buying channels of these factors will influence the consumer to do the final decision to choose to buy which kind of product in the consumption market. Also, any retailers need to concern whether which is the major influence of attribute to the product. Because wrong evaluation of the major attribute of the product will influence the consumer to make final buying decision when who compares the retailer's product to other retailers whose similar products in the consumer's choice process.

How can economical environment factor predict consumers consumption?

The dominant approach to industrial economics is
the one which is usually described as the structure-conduct-performance approach. So, predicting the performance of an industry in terms of profitability and advertising growth can predict consumer consumption in possible. The structure of an industry covers factors like the relative and size of firms, involved the ease of entry into the industry and the elasticity of demand for the output of that industry. The conduct of firms covers the objectives of the firms, price setting behavior, and attitudes to competitors (actual and potential), and from that the performance of that industry predicted, particularly in respect of profitability.

What are the main features of the structure of an industry? Many consumption psychologists discuss on the structure-conduct-performance topic, the number and relative size of the firms and the extent of barriers to entry into the industry to influence the product suppliers to consumption choices in the market. The number and relative size of firms is usually placed under either the size distribution of firms or individual concentration. Most industries don't fit into the category of a large number of small firms or of one firm.

Barriers to entry into an industry comprise all the factors which lead to new entrants into the industry being at a disadvantage to the existing firms because consumers have more choices to buy the similar products from the competitors . The first factor is the existence of economies of scale which means that a new entrant would have to produce on a relatively large scale increasingly. The second factor, the brand of products are supplied by a significant amount and thereby depressing price a significant amount , differentiation and advertising, so that a new entrant has to incur costs to overcome the loyalty of consumers to existing products. A third factor is the ability of existing firms to produce and distribute at lower costs than new entrants. Although, for example, access to cheaper new materials, accumulated knowledge of the industry etc. So, these external marketing environment factor will influence consumption behavior choices. For example, if the industrial structure determines or influences performance, the governments concerned with aspect of industrial performance (particularly aspects like price changes, technological progress and employment levels).

Consumption psychologists have often been assigned that the level of concentration in an industry is largely technological determined and that increases in concentration reflect impact of technological advance with increase the desired size of factory or firm. For example, mobile phone manufacturing industry, if the brand of mobile phone manufacturer had technological advance to manufacture any new model to attract consumers have more buying choices from their mobile products. Then, technological factor will influence consumers have more choices to buy the brand of mobile phone products. Other some psychologists believe the way in which unit costs change with the scale of production (cost conditions and economies of scale) factor which can influence consumers choice behaviors. When public policy favor active industrial intervention to change industrial structures, some indication is required as to whether the minimum efficient scale is small or large relative to the total market to supply their product numbers to influence consumers' behaviors. In the former case a policy favoring small units would be indicated, whereas, in the latter case large units may be favored.

Increasing returns to scale and economies of scales are usually defined as a situation when all inputs into the productive process are increased in the same proportion the volume of output increases in a greater proportion . How can economies of scale influence products supplying numbers? For example, that is the scale of output increases the degree of capital intensity rises. But within that change the type of the capital equipment is likely to be varied. Further, the balance between skilled and unskilled or between manual and non-manual labor may change. Thus , it is necessary to adopt a view of both increasing and decreasing returns.

The definition of unit costs of output declining with increased output. This must refer to all costs(including capital costs, and can only relate to a particular set of relative prices for inputs from which the unit costs are calculated. It would include any change in the price of input usage, such as mobile phone products which need to use different materials to manufacture any mobile phone products Thus, if a mobile phone firm had to pay more wages as its use of labor increased, that would have to be included. It is generally assumed that, for any scale of output, the firm is combining the impacts in an efficient manner. This efficiency includes economies efficiency (choosing the least cost combinations of inputs) and technical efficiency (producing the maximum feasible output from given inputs). The measurement of returns to scale under this definition may be only relevant to a particular economy, as it depends upon the particular relevance prices used.

Such as, each mobile phone product price will influence consumer individual behavior of choice to buy only one among the different brands of model mobile phones. So, mobile phone manufacturers need to concern how to reduce cost to gain economies of scale input to raise mobile phone output. For example, from a reduction in the effective price of an input to the model of mobile phone, as the volume of the styles of mobile phones purchases increased arising from an increase in monopsony power. For example, three mobile phone plants, A, B, C are assumes to have a fixed mobile phones output, and initially produce with unit costs A1, B1, and C1. Respectively. Supposing plants A and C would make subnormal profits and plant B super-normal profits, when capital costs are based on the historical cost of the mobile phone plant. Now the capital values of plants A and C are, it is argued, unlikely to fall and that of plant B to rise , for the amount which another mobile phone firm could be prepared to pay for a plant will reflect its profit prospects. If the decline in capital value fully reflects the initial deviations for normal profits, unit costs shift to A2, B2 and C2 respectively. Thus, there is a tendency at work towards mobile phone constant unit costs being observed. How far this tendency operates depends upon the based on which mobile phone firms value their assets. When the value is based on historic cost, the tendency does not operate. But the tendency does operate when the value is based in some way on the assets' profit prospects. Thus product manufacturers need to concern how to earn economic of scale to cost to avoid each product price will be changed often to influence consumer choices to other competitors more easily.

How can auctions or online experimentation respond to predict consumer behavior and sale forecast accuracy?

Nowadays, in UK suggests that consumer buying behavior has changed significantly. Consumers caan buying different things, at different times and through different channels. As a result, forecast accuracy is very poor and many companies feel automated forecasting systems can not predict buying behavior more accuracy and relying on analysts to predict buying behavior by psychological methods. Automated forecasting systems weaknesses are such as: Historical data alone can't be used to predict feature sales in times and drawing together a wider range of internal and external data would help improve forecast accuracy. The impact on revenue manager varies widely. When sales forecasts are important, adjustments to revenue management system outputs are needed to retain credibility. When customers' behavior are poor to understand, there may be a need to sell from auctions or online experimentation to predict the market response. So, these automated forecasting system have these weaknesses to cause companies feel technological method can not be better than psychological method to predict further consumption behavior for whose products.

In psychological consumption of prediction view point, learning how to predict changes in consumers' attitudes and behaviors which is important to any companies. For example, in part behavior has changes as a result a recent major disruptive events, such as recession and exchange rate changes etc. economic factor, but there are other non economic factors to change consumers' attitudes and behaviors. For example, consumers are becoming smarter in their use of the internet to research products based on previous customers' view, seek out the best, deals and offers and then buy online, with a corresponding increase in the number of price comparison sites. So , companies are percentage seeing the rise of the strategic consumer who observes the dynamic of supplier pricing and adapts their buying strategy in response. However, some observers suggest that these changes to consumers' attitudes and behaviors are fundamental long, lasting and likely to continue to be disruptive.

Some consumption psychologists feel sales have become less predictable. In general, sales forecasts based on historical patterns in time series have become less accurate and hence less useful in the past year in many industries, not just these traditionally served by revenue management. Does forecast accuracy easily? For some revenue managers may be not too much, in some businesses prices are set by reference to the main competitors and forecasts have limited impact on operating and decisions about capacity. Marketing forecasting is aim to setting prices, maximizing revenue and managing operations.

However, forecast accuracy is very important to find why changing consumer attitudes and the implications for customer segmentation and forecasting of buying behaviors are not just relevant to revenue management. They are also fundamental to sales, marketing , brand management, customer loyalty, product design and beyond. Perhaps it has an opportunity for revenue managers to take a lead in influencing thinking of their colleagues in these areas. Some consumption psychologists forecast the future, who concern the historical data of companies collection before the recession, it can no longer be applied to forecast consumer behavior during the recession or after. At the opposite extreme, companies can simply continue to between auto prediction system to predict when the market stability will return soon and how to influence consumer behavior.

Sales are likely to depend on the economic situation, the competition and consumer behavior. However, these are external environmental factor to influence consumption of behavior. If it is possible to separate out these effects, then the forecasting model can take account of them by either building the economy/market into the model or segmenting consumers in an economy/market invariant way. External data, for example on the economic situation can also provide a good indicator of future sales. For example, internet (online) web site research technology is one possibility for combining and processing data from different sources on the web using automated tools. If buying behavior is changing and every consumer demand is becoming elastic, not only to increase revenue, but also to improve knowledge of the customers. For example, online auctions are mainly used in the travel and hospitality industries for offloading surplus capacity have been shown when facing only uncertain consumer demand. However, analyzing external economy environment factor is not effective to minimize risk to the sellers. Because sale forecasts are never going to be completely accurate and there is an argument for moving the focus away from being smarter with existing data towards making the business less dependent on sale forecasts. For example, taking close look at increasing flexibility in the supply chain or operations or re-examine the strategy for setting price.

What the current situation really emphasizes however is that there is certainly a need for forecast accuracy to be taken seriously by revenue managers and reported on by revenue management system. Thus, revenue managers need to concern how to predict whose consumers' psychological emotions to find why the reasons can influence whose consumption attitudes and behaviors changing to cause their product sale numbers had been falling. So, it seems that consumers' emotions can be influenced whose buying behavior by online auctions factor.

Apply knowledge management method to predict Walt Disney entertainment theme park behavioral consumption

6.1 Disney market research method

Introduction

How apply psychology methods to predict behavioral consumption to earn economic benefit. I shall indicate how to apply psychological methods to assist enterprises to predict what are clients' preferable choices to increase more attractive effort to win competitors. Enterprises include Walt Disney entertainment theme park how it applied knowledge management psychological method to attract more visitors ; Universities why need to consider campus building location and course teaching methods to attract students' choices ; airlines why need to consider how flight gas or oil price influences to passengers' choices ; underground train enterprises why need to consider route location influences to passengers' transportation choices ; Finally, environment protection product firms why need to consider what environment pollution benefits to society to influence businessmen decide to buy environment protection products of choices.

In behavioral economy view point, I shall indicate health food consumers' consumption behaviors are similar to Disney entertainment theme paek visitors' consumption behaviors. Concerning health food consumers who will prefer to choose health foods to eat more than unhealth goods. Their consumption behaviors are similar to Disney visitors' consumption behavior. Expecting to spend less time to queue of Disney visitors who only prefer to choose the entertainment facilities to play which only need them to spend less time to queue in Disney theme park. So, their consumption behaviors concern behavioral economy theory. Such as , the Disney expecting short time queue time of visitors who expect to spend less time to queue in order to play any many Disney entertainment facilities. In economic behavior view point, Disney visitors will feel queue time is same to money, who feel to wait long time to play any entertainment facilities in queue, who will feel to pay tickets to enter Disney, the ticket prices are not reasonable and unfair to them.

In economic behavior view point, for health food consumers, who will feel waste money to spend any unhealth foods to eat. Excess weight is significant societal problems, mindfulness may encourage healthier weight and eating habits. Some health psychologists found a positive relation between mindfulness and healthier eating. It causes some consumers concern health eating behavior, such as reduced calorie consumption and healthier snack choices, who also find causal effect of mindfulness healthier eating who found evidence that mindfulness is affected eating behavior by encouraging attitude preferences for generic mindfulness-based strategies which could have benefits for encouraging healthier eating behavior.

Excessive weight has several causes including physical inactivity, over-consumption of convenient food behavior. Mindful people experience their environments allow positive and negative thoughts and feelings to occur with less judgement. Mindfulness is associated with better mental health, relationship satisfaction and self regulation (Brown et al , 2007). Self regulation strength way, however play a role in other contents. Where mindful individuals face greater temptation, unhealthy eating may often result from a lack of self-regulations, which should be reduced by mindfulness. Thus, any one habit health eating behavior consumer will concern to choose what kind of health food to buy only choice health food to eat. So, it has limit health food demand to this habit health eating behavior consumer. Otherwise, any one inhabit health eating behavior consumer won't have any limit food choice. So, a variety of food demand is much to inhabit health eating behavior consumer to compare to habit health eating behavior consumer as well as a health food choice will be the concerning health food consumers' economic behavior model (attitude).

Walt Disney entertainment thems park had ever applied psychological methods to find what factors had caused its visitor numbers to be decreased. As Harriet Griffey (2010) stated that "sometimes, boredom can give disadvantages to reduce staffs' ability to motive to work and reduces positive emotion , such as happiness. Thus, it causes people (staffs) lack motivated reasoning to unconsciously evaluate evidence in ways consistent with whose preferences. This type of bias can hinder a company's ability to learn from mistakes and to build successful strategies." However, Disney needed to implement knowledge management strategy to satisfy visitors demand after who entered .Disney demanded cleaners to repeat to remember any information to prepare to answer visitors' enquiries. It will train every cleaner memory to remember any information to be long term from short term memory successfully and every cleaner won't feel bore to do only cleaning job duty. When every one feel places are clean, who will concentrate on answering any visitors enquiries as the same time. Even, if they can give excellent service performance to serve visitors to let who to know how to go to any places in the short time. It is possible that visitors will appreciate whose service performance to let their manager to know, so that every cleaner will have chance to raise salary. Besides, waiting time and queues are daily problem for Disney theme park. Fast lines or priority queues appear as a solution of efficient queues for clients. Disney understood fast ticket line system affected visitor attendance numbers. Disney entertainment facilities long waits leaded to lower service evaluations and greater customer dissatisfaction. Efficient queue waiting time management can improve Disney visitor satisfaction and the willingness to recommend the service. Disney analysed of theme park visitor behaviour in relation to pay the higher ticket price to select to pay more for fast queuing line ticket than common queuing line ticket. In fact, Disney fast queuing line ticket system choice gave potential queues to any waiting clients . In general, Disney visitors don't like to wait long time in every entertainment facilities queuing line, who will feel a waste of time and waiting can lead to negative emotional response like frustration, impotence, tension or irritation .In fact, Disney amusement theme park needed visitors wait long queues and delays which were a frequent occurrence in every entertainment facilities line. Disney theme park as sets of rides, spectacles and leisure mechanisms are intended to entertainment and spark the imagination of clients, allowing visitors to escape their daily routing. In result, waiting is often a problematic issue that can influence Disney visitor experience and that can appear as one of the principal motives for complaining. As Disney visitor demand fluctuates constantly and demand patterns are often difficult to predict. It caused extra staff needed for the extra line. Finally, priority services such as fast line system facilities segmentation of its amusement park. When Disney offer the possibility of purchases a fast line, which are creating two different group. Disney visitors who are highly sensitive to waiting times are willing to pay to avoid or reduce lines or visitors that are highly sensitive to price that prefer to wait rather than to pay extra money. Also, Disney provides extensive training opportunity for participants through its own Disney university. The question of whether their training opportunity can lead the improve human resource activities. On the third hand problem, Disney are also worried that employees may leave it and join other competitor to serve their parks after training. Disney shows a trend of increasing depending on human capital other than physical capital. It thinks human capital is the knowledge, skills, ideas and commitment of its employees. It explains that investing in training and development is essential to its client service growth. In fact, Disney had owned enough entertainment facilities, restaurants, hotels, shopping centres within theme park, but its visitor numbers are increasing to need to be served satisfactorily. However, it needs to train cleaners, entertainment facilities service staffs, queuing service staffs, hotels, restaurants, shopping centres service staffs, instead of it's entertainment facilities attraction.

Disney observes that spending on training and development is typically regarded as consumption, instead of investment. On job training usually can't be replaced by formal education, therefore Disney chooses to make contribution on providing further training and development to employees. Disney paid salary for staff training, which included classroom, seminars, symposia or conferences; computer based training, on site training, book and periodicals reading, formal mentoring and informal mentoring program opportunities to meet its old staffs and new staffs both needs of motivate factors to achieve advancement , achievement, personal growth responsibility and achievement and recognition to raise its business performance effectively and efficiently. However, Disney's amount of training has a positive influence on intrinsic motivation of its employees. Job satisfaction, salary, working condition, its policies, administration, relationship with supervisors, peers and subordinates are Disney factors to influence it's human resource activities performance. Disney training contents include these functional area: Raising excellent service performance include that hotel food and beverage service delivery, shopping center, merchandise sale, restaurant service, entertainment facilities queuing waiting service, cleaning and enquiring how to go different locations in Disney, cashier service etc. They are very important to influence visitor numbers. Disney implementation of knowledge management solution to improve queuing waiting line process. The use of Disney front line service staffs as human capital combined with knowledge of customer preference has made the fast pass an innovation solution to enhance queuing in the Disney theme parks. Disney ability to capture customers in virtual queues when giving them a pleasurable waiting experience has made them a leader in knowledge management initiatives in the service industry. Disney's emphasis on human capital within their theme parks, combined with traditional queuing theory to create more pleasurable waiting environments. Hence, Disney showed the value of tacit employee knowledge integrated with traditional queuing theory to reduce loss of customer satisfaction to enhance, goodwill and profitability. Knowledge management expresses itself as human action in form of evaluation, attitudes, points of view, commitments, motivation etc. It seemed that Disney agreed that human capital (people, knowledge, ideas, creativity) maybe today's most valuable commodity.

Knowledge Management Strategy was used to queue control from Disney. Disney managers have long understand the pressure of waiting time and revenue; who know that every minutes spent waiting in queuing is a minute that the client is not generating revenue. So, Disney managers have processed with design of a reservation system recognizes that guests can be freed from physically standing in the actually and perception of waiting by allowing guests to engage has arrived. Cope et al., (2008) showed that" the system was first tested at Disney in 1998. Managers assessed the system by surveying guests who used it. Results were positive and indicated that guests spent substantially less time in queuing, spent more per capita, and saw significantly more attractions, satisfaction level sky rocketed.The system was expanded in 1999 to include five of the most popular park attractions and was named FASTPASS. The system has since been expanded to all Disney theme parks worldwide, and is now in use by over 50 million guests per year .That guests have two options .Namely, they can choose to Obtain a FASTPASS ticket and come back a later, designed time or Wait in a traditional queuing. Guests are assisted in making their choice by information regarding estimated waits of both options. Thus, can decide to wait in the traditional queuing, or take a FASTPASS ticket and return it a later time with no further wait. Once an assigned FASTPASS time is generated and provided to a guest, it is valid for the 60 minutes beyond that time, creating a window in which guest can return."
There are numerous benefits in allowing park guests to return to an attraction within a designed time frame. Queue Waits involve managing two major client issues:

1.How long Disney visitors actually wait every time queue.

2.How long Disney visitor think they are waiting by whose psychological feeling every time queue.

Thus, if they feel that who spend much time to queue, it will cause they feel angry and they also feel admission ticket price is paid too high to them unfairly. In general, clients were allowed the ability to see two attractions during the time they would have previously been able to see only one. This can viewed as an implementation of a multi-phased system, depending on the attraction picked, each queuing may be single channel attractions, the guest creates whose own multi phase system. Obvious, results, were that guests were able to engage in more revenue producing activities, saw more of the popular attractions and began to par take care, in other less utilized attractions . Wiig defined(1993)" Knowledge management in different ways and from different perspective. The emphasis is on human know how and how it brings value to an organization. Intangible asset contributes to corporation objective may be immeasurable and isn't simple to evaluate the impacts of knowledge management." However, Knowledge management may not be only factor influencing organizational performance. In fact, Disney refined technology utilization to improve the user design of all human resource related systems, improving timeliness (queue waiting time deduction), setting elapsed time goals and monitor performance towards those standards, considering to use of automated fast queue waiting system, evaluating staffing levels, a close examination of adequacy of current staff level is warranted, beyond to improve visitors satisfaction. Clients holding fast pass tickets may choose to visit a gift shop or any park concessions. Thus, Disney has ability to co-branded products and service. Disney's approach combining queuing and human capital. Dunn, J et al., (2002) showed "The use of fast pass provides an insightful application of the combination of techniques of queuing and human capital to strategically leverage knowledge management principle .When waiting lines are an part of the Disney experience, park guests build magical memories through innovation. It is Disney's recognition of front line service staffs that transforms that employees into knowledge who multi task in their roles.For example, an attraction host or a street sweeper may be a valuable Source knowledge to park guests. In addition to their primary roles, they may have a wealth of information about attractions for guests. They may be able to give directions, provide schedules, and offer helpful suggestions from their daily observation. This is the first stop to increase knowledge management . Next, Disney improves its clients' perception by minimizing the perception of waits. The use of the fast pass enables Disney not only to enhance the psychological aspect of waiting lines, but also to capitalize at the same time." Instead, Disney needed to give people specific tools designed to help them to do their job and solve specific business problems. Thus, after Disney learned how it applied the knowledge management method to solve its challenges, e.g. Human capital and queuing theory provide two very different valuable assets to raise its competitive abililty. Then, its visitor numbers was increasing largely and quickly.

It seems Disney understand what which visitor's individual psychological needs, who needs to pay reasonable ticket fee and who also dislike to need to wait long time to queue to play any entertainment facilities. Disney also understand cleaners have extra time to serve visitors when who can answer any visitor individual enquiries immediately. After the cleaners will feel satisfactory and happy if who can give positive feedback from any visitor individual enquiry. The cleaner will feel more valuable to Disney employer, due to who can do any enquiry duty during whose working hours. The most important, who have chance to get higher salary and promotion. Thus, Disney can predict visitor and staff individual psychological needs, then it can raise new and keep old visitor numbers and keep old staffs to choose to stay to it's organization to work for long term. It can earn more economic benefit for long term after it can predict whose staffs and visitors whose psycholgical needs successfully.

Why will decisions under uncertainty cause? In consumer choice process, who has chance to encounter decisions under uncertainty. For example, the attributes of each product were assumed to be known with certainty. Thus, the consumers knew the price, picture, quality, reliability and visual appeal of each product type. All consumers need to do was to be importance weights and subjective values to these attributes and then derive a weighted average. In many of choice alternatives are not known with certainty ahead of time. Often, the outcomes are produced by decision depend on the state of the world at the time and the decision is made. For another example, a LCD television can produce a high -definition picture only of the service providers transmit high-definition programs. To take this uncertainty into account, the consumer has to judge not only the value of a high-definition display , but also the likelihood that this attribution will be available.

Perhaps, more readily recognized are the risks and uncertainties inherent in investment decisions. The investment outcomes of a decision to invest in a fixed interest certificate of deposit or a stock market mutual fund depend on future market conditions. Whereas the CD produces a known payoff over a given time period, the amount and probability of possible gains or losses to be expected of the mutual fund can only be estimated.

Thus, advertising can reduce decision uncertainty to consumers' choices. If the product advertising can attract to consumer's consideration , it will persuade the consumer to choose to buy the brand of product. Clearly, information about the decision making process, in general, as well as about decisions of particular relevance to consumer behavior. Thus, it seems advertising information can reduce consumers' choices processes under uncertainty to decide to buy the brand of product preference choice.

Why businessmen need to divide customer segment(s) to decide who is target customer group to predict consumer behavior. Nowadays, consumers are unique in themselves. A comprehensive knowledge of consumers and their consumption behavior is essential for a firm to succeed. In order to understand and predict consumption patterns and behaviors within segment(s), market research becomes essential.

Why businessmen need to concern market research with consumer behavior. Each individual is unique himself/ herself and needs and wants vary from person to person. Markets identify segments and target one or few of these segments and target one or few of these segments and thereby fulfil the qualifications of the marketing concept. First, marketers need to identify customer needs and wants and then, deliver product and service offering, so as to satisfy the customers more efficiently and effectively, than the competitors.

Such as Disney, in order to understand and predict each visitor consumption pattern and behavior within segment(s), e.g. young, adult, old age, rich and poor segment. It seems Disney has many different age , student or working people customer segments. So, market research becomes essential to assist Disney to predict what different market segment needs. Such as young age segment needs excitement, e.g. entertainment facilities to play . Otherwise, old age segment needs not excitement entertainment facilities , this old age segment needs to walk in Disney garden or go to shopping centre or sit down to watch Disney movies etc. not excitement activites to. Market research defines to gather information about market and the customers. The environment of a firm, such as Disney may be grouped as the micro and macro environment both. The micro environment firm comprises forces to close affect the firm directly. For example, the firm's internal environment, the founder/leader and whose vision and mission, clients, competitors, suppliers and channel intermediaries. The macro environment, on the other hand, companies forces in the environment that first affect the micro environment and thought that which affect the firm, in other words, which affect the firm indirectly, including the demographic factors, socio-economic factors, political factors, technological factors, cultural factors, natural factors etc. The micro environment is studied in terms of strength(s) and weakness and when the macro environment is studied in terms of opportunities and threat(s) analysis of both comprises the SWOT analysis.

Thus, Disney market research can help which to understand the specific marketing situation facing . Identifies the needs and wants of Disney different age client segment(s), identifies variables age target segment(s), serves them better through formulation of appropriate marketing strategies a mix of the 4(p)s. It's goal is to achieve maximum efficiency and effectiveness to meet customer needs and wants and client satisfaction . Thus is obtained through a conscious attempt at understanding " what" the disney young or old age target needs, "why" who needs, "when" who needs, from "where" who needs, "how" much who needs and "how" often who needs during who are staying in Disney theme park at the staying time. Thus, the integration of Disney market research with Disney visitors behavior: Disney marketing research can understand and predict any different age segment behavior as well as Disney consumer research is a process and tools to be used to study what consumer behavior is or who expect to buy when Disney visitors are staying in Disney theme park.

Marketing research objective is to study the marketing environment and the clients who are a part of it, as well as to study consumers as individuals as groups. It focuses to establish trends and identify opportunities and threats in the environment, to study the market and forecast potential and to predict buying patterns based on modeling and , to understand consumption behavior and consumption patterns. Besides, consumer behavior research has tradition approach and current approach has traditional approach and current approach.

Traditional approach divides positivist and interpretivist both approaches. Positivist approach refers to as modernism is the earliest approach to studying consumer behavior and trends the study as an applied science. It lays emphasis on the causes of consumer behavior, these causes are directly related to effects. Thus it treats consumer as "rational" human things, who make purchase decisions after collecting information and weighing all alternatives. The process of consumer decision making, it seems of rationality, rational decision making and problem solving is the key. It is based on certain assumption, consumer actions based on cause and effect relationship can be generalized, who can be objectively measured and tested. If researchers could identify the reasons behind consumption behavior, who would be able to predict it, and if who could predict consumer behavior, who could influence it.

The methods focus on prediction of client behavior, including surveys, observations and experiments. It aims at drawing conclusions a large samples. The positivist consumer actions can be objectively measured and tested. It focuses to predict consumer behavior, e.g. large samples of quantitative methodology. Otherwise, the interpretivist consumer action is a cause and effect relationship can't be generalized , consumption pattern and behaviors are unique, these are unpredictable. Consumer actions are unique and different both between two consumers, and/or within the same consumer at different times and situations. It can't be objectively measured, tested and generalized. It focuses the act of understanding the consumption rather than predicting the act of purchase, e.g. methodology small samples of qualitative methodology.

In consumption psychological view point, the current approach is the term " dialectics" , considers all forms of human behavior, thus the current approach to the study of consumer divided into four approaches: materialism approach implies that consumer behavior is shaped by the material environment, e.g. money, possessions etc. , change approach means consumer behavior is " dynamic" in nature, it is always in a process of continuous motion, transformation and change. Totality means consumption behavior is " interconnected" with other forms of human contradiction means views changes in consumer behavior as arising from their internal contradictions, like moods, emoting etc. The approach studies the consumer as a complex total whole and views consumer purchase as well as consumption processes.

The current approach to studying consumer behavior uses both the quantitative as well as qualitative approaches. There are three broad research perspectives in consumer behavior: they are as follows:

Decision making perspective, the experiment perspective and behavioral influence perspective. According to decision making perspective , the buying process is a sequential in nature, with the consumer perceiving that there exists a problem and that moving across a series of logical and rational steps to solve the problem; stages being problem recognition, information search, evaluation of alternatives , purchase decision and past purchase behavior, it emphasizes rational , logical and cognitive approach to consumer decision making and purchase process.

The experiential perspective believes that not all buying may be rational and logical, in some cases, buying results are from a consumers' desire for fun and fantasy, pleasures, emotions and moods. The perspective emphasizes that consumers are feelers as well as thinkers. The behavioral influence perspective holds that forces in the environment stimulate a consumer to make purchases without developing beliefs and attitudes about the product.

In general, quantitative research is used by the positivists and qualitative research is used by interpretivists. How to use quantitative research in consumer behavior? It comprises (i) research techniques that are used to gather quantitative data over large samples randomly and (ii) statistical tools and techniques, e.g. survey, observation and experiments techniques. Thus type of research is descriptive in nature. It is primarily used by the positivists when studying consumer behavior with a focus on prediction of consumer behavior and techniques are also used by " dialectics" approach.

How to use qualitative research in consumer behavior? It comprises (i) research techniques that are used to gather quantitative data over small samples techniques , e.g. depth interviews, focus group of study is subjective in nature. The focus is on understanding consumption behavior and consumption pattern . the objective is to gain an understanding of consumer behavior and the causes marketing situations are unique, and hence the finding can't be generalized to marketing situations. It is primarily used by the interpretivists when studying consumer behavior. However, the qualitative techniques are also used by " dialectics" approach.

Today, both approaches and are used to study consumer behavior. In some causes, qualitative research may act as an indicator to qualitative research through case studies and other qualitative measures. Qualitative research is very often a prelude to quantitative research are used to prepares scales for surveys and experiments.

Brand image attention of behavioral consumption of prediction method

Brand is one good behavioral economy method to persuade Disney consumption. Disney can apply brand image prediction method to attract visitors visiting choice. Disney is one famous entertainment theme park in the World. The application of disney visitor consumption psychology, and in particular to Disney branding, has gained popularity over the past decade in academic research and business practice. What neuroscience can bring to advance Disney entertainment theme park understanding of the consumer psychology of brands choice of behavioral consumption. The Disney brand preference formation over time has four basic components: (1) representation and attention, (2) predicted value , (3) experienced value and (4) remembers value and learning.

First, on representation and attention component, it means that the amount of information consumers are exposed to is enormous, yet consumer's processing capacity is limited. How Disney consumers represent, attend to, and perceive incoming information may have a profound influence on their behavioral consumption , i.e. Disney brand identification. Representation is the first process in entertainment theme park industry brand decisions , which involves forming the representation of the choice alternatives, that is brand identification. For example, different beer brands provide different options for choice are identified to consumers. At the same time, the entertainment theme park consumer needs to integrate information on internal state , (e.g. thirst level) and external states , e.g. (location , social context) that drive attention. For example, when faced with a choice between a entertainment theme park consumer's choice is likely to depend on whose own level of entertainment theme park playing facilities (an internal state) and level of entertainment facilities chooses to play (an external state). However, the entertainment theme park brand image is a visual system allows for rapid entertainment theme park brand and entertainment service performance identification. One of the key questions at this stage is what entertainment theme park consumers pay attention to (i.e. focus on) once who are exposed to a number of rapidly identified entertainment theme park choice alternatives (i.e. theme park images).

Attention is the mechanism responsible for selecting the information that gains preferential status above other available information for researching on entertainment theme park image. Thus, if the entetainment theme park brand image is attractive, then it will be probable attract the initial eye movement of entertainment theme park consumers and thus may have a profound effect on related theme park consumer behavior. For example, Pieters and Wedel (2007) showed that ensuring that consumers pay attention to the brand displayed in a print ad. It is the most effective way to ensure that who will transfer their attention to other elements of the print ad. So, entertainment theme park image of attractive visual selection and eye movement can enhance the quality of incoming information to consumer individual behavioral consumption for the entertainment theme park of choice. The suggestion of eye-tracking is as a useful tool for determining the extent to which entertainment theme park consumers find different entertainment facilities images extensions plausible. In sum, representation and attention are complex processes that influence all subsequent steps in our brand decisions framework.

Next, the step is predicted value, it is of each (entetainment theme park image) brand that is available for choice to represent the entertainment theme park consumer's belief about the experienced value of that brand at same time in the future. In other words, the predicted values involves the consumer's evaluation of how much enjoyment who will desire form playing theme park facilities among of different theme park of entertainment service choice. For example, clothes are at different retail stores (e.g. H&M vs. Zara), consumer who are loyal to a store as measured by real purchasing behavior. (i.e. amount spent, frequency and recent of purchases based on loyalty card data) show more activation in the compared to consumers who are less loyal. The cloth brand inviting loyalty card holders who will be persuaded by the brand . So, the loyalty card of the brand, e.g. Disney loyalty card of park's visitors can be the predicted value to the Disney image of the entertainment facilities to persuade the Disney loyalty card holders to choose to pay admission fee to enter Disney theme park to play.

Next, the step is experienced value , it is based on the pleasure derived from consuming a brand, such as Disney entetainment facilities service. It is a concept of motivational value to the consumer. Motivational value is a concept that is related to how predicted and experienced values interact is the motivational value or incentive of an option to the consumer. So building good brand image memory us important to influence consumer psychology. For example, the information of channel ,.e.g. ad. can build brand image memory to consumer more easily. Thus, good brand image can build good memory to consumers to prefer to choose to buy the brand of product easily. Otherwise, bad brand image can build bad memory to consumers to not prefer to choose to buy the brand of product easily. Thus, manufacturers or sellers can not neglect how to build good brand image to attract any consumer individual attention by attrative advertising because good brand image has close relationship with psychological consumption for shopping. It seems brand loyalty of famous degree can help businessmen to predict whether consumers are accepting or are not accepting to choose to buy their products or consume their service provision more accurate. For example, if the product brand is very famous long term, it seems consumers are accepting to choose to buy the product. Otherwise, if the product brand is not famous long term, it seems consumers are not ccepting to choose to buy the product.

Can scientific research method predict Disney visitors behavior ?

Using scientific research methods to predict Disney consumption behavior phenomena in this field, some experts had attempted to do research in predictive validity to evaluate whether a measure of scientific achievement to consumer behavior. There are three groups thought to have varying knowledge of and ability to predict consumer behavior are academics, marketing practitioners and consumers in general. Academic groups use their scientific knowledge of consumer behavior as a basic for such activities as teaching, consulting for corporations, and testifying in legal and regulatory proceedings. In contrast, marketing practitioners are likely to be as familiar with this scientific literature. However, practitioners gain expertise through their experience. This expertise might help them to make accurate predictions of consumer behavior. Finally, when few studies on consumer behavior reach the general public, consumer's personal experiences should help them to predict certain aspects of customer behavior. So, it seems that whether Disney ought choose to do consumer behavioral psychological method to predict consumer behavior, such as personal experiences (psychological feeling) method is more accurate than to scientific method, such as marketing research method.

In this discussion, I shall imply two hypotheses about why Disney experts ought measure consumer behavior by behavioral psychological method predictions more than scientistic method, such as marketing research method . The first hypothesis, experts can make more accurate predictions than novices as well as the second hypothesis, academics can make more accurate predictions them practitioners. Thus, these hypotheses bring the questions and asked the subjects to predict whether each hypothesis tended to be true or false. For example, whether the more frequently an adolescent interacts with peers about consumption matters is the greater the tendency to use peer preferences in evaluating products? (Moschis & Moore, 1979). Will a person be more satisfied with their recently purchased car if the car met or exceeded whose expectations? (Westbrook 1980). Hence, using behavioral psychological prediction method , it will ask these these questions to gather the data to attempt to analyze what factors can influence whose satisfied feeling during who play any Disney entertainment facilties. These survey questions can include: Will a disney visitor feel more satisfied to play any Disney entertainment facilities with who recently visited Disney if the Disney entertainment facilities met or exceed whose expectation? Whether the more frequently Disney entertainment facilities a player with whose friends who have more satisfied feeling to play any Disney entertainment facilities to compare the less frequently Disney entertainment facilities another player alone or no any friend?

A long term survey research indicated that a consumer reserch result for the practitioner group, who worked with marketing problems, but who were unlikely to be familiar with scientific research on consumer behavior. For example, systematic sampling was used to select 100 practitioners from the 1984 year American Marketing Association Membership Directory (academic addresses were excluded), a self addresses envelope was enclosed in the original mailings, and two postcard reminders were sent. Replies were received from 20 academics and 13 practitioners.

Subjects were asked whether who had previously read each of the studies. Two academic had read most of the studies because few of their predictions were usable (three or fewer), all responses from these subjects were excluded. Two academic respondents said that who did not understand all of the hypotheses, so who were also excluded. This left 16 academics. Other practitioner was excluded because who said that who did not understand the instructions, which reduced the number of practitioners to 12. Six academics and one practitioner reported reading one or more studies and their responses for these studies were excluded. Finally, the predictions by expects and native subjects showed that the prediction of consumer research percentage is larger than academics experts. For example, by assuming that researchers typically found what who were looking for and as a result, predicting " true" for all hypotheses a subject would have been correct for 74.2% of the predictions, subjects who gave a higher percentage of these answers would be expected to achieve higher level of accuracy. Thus, consumption psychological prediction method is more effective to compare marketing research. Such as Disney entertainment theme park needs to use psychological method to predict whose visitor consumption behavior to gather what the factors can influece whose satisfied feeling to be poor after who played Disney entertainment facilities. Otherwise, in general marketing research method can only find its similar theme park competitors' strengths and weaknesses, so this method can not get the actual Disney visitors' feeling more easily.

Can intentions Disney visitor behavior be predicted by survey research ?

How can be survey research measured that is applicable to intentions, attitude or satisfaction data to predict consumer behavior? Whether surveyed consumers will be predicted how consumers behavior are more easier than non surveyed consumers. Most academic studies of satisfaction use consumers' intention to repurchase as the criterion variable (for an exception, see Bolton 1998), and most companies rely on consumers' purchase intentions to forecast their adoption of new products or the repeat purchase of existing ones (Jamieson and Bass 1989).

In practice, some consumer psychologists' studies adjust the intention scores by analyzing that actual purchase behavior of consumers whose purchase intentions have been measured previously. For example, the popular ACNIELSEN BASES model forecasts aggregate purchase rates by applying conversion rates to measured purchase intentions (e.g. it seems that 75% of consumers who checked the top purchase-intentions box will actually purchase the product). To obtain these conversion rates, BASES uses previous studies that measured the purchase intentions of consumers and then tracked their actual purchases. However, investigating whether survey research is useful to measure consumer behavior. It has a weak point, a limitation of these studies is that companies (businessmen) focus on the internal rather than the external accuracy of purchase-intention measures. That is, the company studies measure the improvement in the ability to forecast the behavior of consumers whose intentions who previously measured for survey research experiments, not the behavior of consumers whose intentions who did not measure. Therefore, the studies assume that the companies can predict the intention-behavior relationship of non-surveyed consumers on the basis of the relationship that surveyed consumer exhibit.

It would suggest that studies measure the strength of the association between intentions and behavior on the same sample of consumers overstate that external predictive accuracy of purchase intentions by survey method. This would explain why so many new products fail even after which are performed well in purchase-intention tests by survey method. I shall suggest survey framework distinguished between two sources of measurement reactivity. The first is self-generated validity effects, it is as a strengthened relationship between latent intentions and behavior, due to the measurement of intentions from post-survey research. The second source includes all measurement effects that are independent of latent intentions, such as those that social norms or post-survey intention modifications create.

I also suggest a two stage procedure to detect whether the act of measurement alters the strength of the relationship between a latent construct that is measured through surveys, experiments or observations and its consequence (e.g. intentions-behavior, attitudes-intentions, attitudes-behavior, satisfaction behavior) and to determine the time relationship in the absence of the difference between non-survey and survey consumers behavior measurement for Disney. For example, prediction of Disney visitor's entertainment facilities choice behavior intention to find why the kind of entertainment facilities can attract more visitors choose to play in Disney theme park. Disney survey method can measure to any machine entertainment facilities. So, Disney can show the strength of the relationship between latent intentions and visitor entertainment facilities choice behavior is stronger for surveyed consumers than for similar non surveyed consumers in order to find the reasons why more visitors choose to play which kind of entertainment facilities.

I also suggest the Disney survey questions can concern to compare with other inputs factors of entertainment facilities choice decisions. e.g. personal entertainment tastes, mood, other similar entertainment theme parks' competitive environment. In order to make subsequent visiting Disney behavior is more than one time with prior intentions for every Disney old visitors. For example, Feldman and Lynch's (1988) survey method predictions, Fitzsimons and Morwitz (1996) found that measurement of general intentions to purchase automobiles increase the likelihood that buyers will repurchase the automobile brand that they also previously consume and that first time buyers will purchase brands will large market shares. Under the assumption, if the survey's result showed the automobiles brand-specific purchase intentions. Thus, Fitzsimons and Morwitz's results suggest that the measurement of general intentions increases the association between latent, brand-specific intent and brand choice. So, brand is a factor which can influence consumers to choose to buy which automobiles. In conclusion, it seems Disney can attempt to use survey method to investigate visitor entertainment facilities choice behavior to predict what factor is the most influential to attract every Disney visitor to choose to play the entertainment as well as what factor is the most influential to every Disney (re-visitor) old visitor to choose to visit Disney theme park again.

6.2 University campus choice and teaching method choice psychological prediction

University campus location factor

University can attempt to predict student individual psychological needs to avoid student turnover numbers increasing and campus location factor can influence students' studying choices. Whether University location can be a competitive advantage to attract students to study? The school (university) location means that the proximity of city center and the proximity of students home. To increase the occupancy rate, the university location is needed to provide as a model and resources based view which will be used to explain why the school location is a kind of competitive advantage for universities. According to Porter theory, it is a part of factor, which has some advantages against the treat of entry. It can decrease the treatment of rivalry. However, a good place has a certainly positive effect for attracting staff and more students. For resource-based view, the location is one of the internal resources for long term economic benefit production of factor. It can be accepted as one of the physical and tangible resource of a university.

I shall apply the first attractive factor of Porter five forces and resource based model to analyze my opinion to explain why school (university location) can influence students to choose the university to study. This view is represented by the opportunities and the threats. The university of thought is the resource based view which is represented by the strengths and weaknesses of the firm. Porter's five force model of competition elements include threats of entrants or substitutes, bargaining power of buyers or suppliers and competition rivalry. A firm's resources include brand name, in-house knowledge of technology, employment of skilled personnel, trade contract, machinery, efficient procedures and capital etc. Such as, both tangible and intangible assets are considered a firm's resources. For a university, customers can be thought as a students, suppliers can be thought as staff. In higher education industry, the good transportation infrastructure and well-connected universities have some advantages against the treat of entry to attract good staff and more students. The place of a university can decrease of treatment of rival and a good place has certainty positive location is an opportunity for universities to attract the students.

The resource based theory of university
location competitive advantage
Students choose any one university to study who will judge whether economic cost is reasonable to decide to study the school, e.g. school fee, transportation cost etc.According to the Porter's theory, the resource based theory can apply competitive resources to be identifies to higher education institutions. For higher education institutions, such as resources might include the reputation of certain departments, the grouping together of areas of specialist expertise and the development of technical patents etc. Also higher education resources may not be imperfectly mobile, as the competitive resources of a university identifies tangible, intangible and organizational assets. So, the tangible resources might include campus location, building capacity, conference facilities and medical research facilities. Intangible resources generally include such items as patents, teaching and research performance, service levels and technology and the geographical location of a service. In a university, such intangible resources might include some of the above and may also include employees/ associates, e.g. experienced professors, renowned authors and distinguished teachers. Also, the location of a university can be accepted as physical and tangible resources of a university. However, I believe location is shown as an important factor to affect the students' university enrolment selection decisions.

To sources of competitive advantages are thought to be the reputation of the institution, the curriculum and educational standards, school fees (tuition), location and student activities etc. different factors. Moreover, any university's general client segments include such as, high school graduates, elderly students and international students, that have been influenced by several factors when selecting the best university to study. One of these factors is again location, the proximity to home and easy transportation is critical factor in selecting a university. Presumably, institutions that are located along well-established public transit routes have a competitive advantage over those with poor transit links. Due to the efficiency of innovation activity increased in easily accessible locations with a high density of economic activity. The existence of education and research institutions as well as easily available information is suggested as a reason for this increase. Also private higher education institutions desire to benefit from these flows by locating itself nearby. Therefore, together with other factors, such as existing capital global flows should be existing capital and population, level of income and location decisions of foundation universities. The location, social life campus, proximity of campus to the city center, exchange programs, the curricula infrastructure, languages medium of instruction and activities are the most significant factors to influence students to choose which university to study. By the past statistic indicated that the location has 94% rate, the proximity of campus to the city center has 84% rate. So, it seems the proximity of campus to the city center factor is more prior choice to compare with the school location is close to the student home factor.

Huang (2012) stated that " the right location attracts more students and ensures the revenues of the institution. The location of an educational institution might influence its future prospect of growth. A good location attracts not only more students, but also excellent teaching staff". Because of job opportunities areas, the students are able to get a part-time job and earn extra money for their tuition (Huang, 2012). Marketing concept has four "P", it can apply to university educational business, such as educational promotion, tuition price, teachers of people and school campus location of place.

Finally, I shall give two assumptions to explain why if the university location is not popular to be accepted to the country's students in general, then it will cause who won't choose to study the university. However, even if the university's tuition is reasonable or cheaper or lecturers are famous or reputation or educational advertisement is attractive. In fact, the poor location factor will influence many local or overseas students who don't choose to study the university in the country. The first assumption is that most of students feel that the proximity of the university to the city center factor affects their university final choice decision and the another assumption is that most of students feel that the proximity of university to home affects their university final choice decision. There two assumptions are used to determine the importance of university location to attract the students. In Porter theory, either proximity of city center and/or proximity of student's home of a university factors have same advantages against the treat of entry. It can decrease the treatment of rival and a good place has certainly positive effect to attract teaching staff and more students. In resource based view, the location can be accepted a kind of internal resources. It can be accepted as one of the sustainable competitive advantages literature, location is a kind of advantage for higher education institutions.

The factor of student demand for alternative modes of course delivery

The factor of student demand for alternative modes of course delivery is another factor to influence the student who chooses the university to study. Any university's educational program includes program design, material production (both print and e-version), promotion, essay competition, school networks, budgeting, coordinating with various constructors, data base management and program evaluation etc.

Nowadays, university teaching methods may include face-to face, online and hybrid modes of course delivery. However, the several ways to students to deliver their course works ,such as full time, part time, internal/ non campus, external studies/distance education, summer school, winter school, semester study and trimester study. The multi site of a university , e.g. major provider of distance online education operates popular affordable learning for student to use internet to study. Although, students do not need to attend to university classroom to listen lecturer's teaching, but it can reduce face-to-face contact between lecturers and students in university classroom often.

Although, it is a technological and innovative and effective learning modalities. In fact, such new technological teaching modalities may be necessitated to the graduated or master degree or doctoral degree students. But, I feel the online teaching method is not suitable to the bachelor degree students. As the delivery of course content or the commoditization of knowledge must be re-thought to the bachelor's if the student can't enquire whose lecturer any questions to give feedback by face-to-face. Then, who will concern the course to feel more difficult possibly if who can't listen whose lecturer's opinion to solve whose challenges about the course any questions immediately in classroom often.

The second attractive factor of student demand for alternative modes of course delivery is another factor to influence the student who chooses the university to study. Nowadays, university teaching method include face to face, online and hybrid modes of course delivery. However, the several ways to students to deliver their coursework, such as full time, part time, internal/on campus, external studies/distance education, "summer school, winter school, semester study and trimester study." The multi site of a university, e.g. major popular provider of distance online education operates a flexible learning for student to use internet to study. It can reduce face to face contact between teachers and students into university classrooms. Although, it is a technological and innovative and effective learning modalities. In fact, such new technological teaching modalities may be necessitated to the graduated students or master degree or doctoral degree students. But, I feel the online teaching method is not suitable to the bachelor degree students. As the delivery of course content or the commoditization of knowledge must be re-thought to the bachelor degree students because whose knowledge level is limited if the student can't ask whose lecturer any questions by face to face contact. So, students will feel difficult to learn if who can't listen whose lecturers' teaching and to enquire any questions and to give feedback in classrooms immediately. It is possible that who will wait long time to ask many questions to prepare to wait lecturers to give feedback by email later if their lecturers use online teaching method. So it is essential that educators and administrators need to understand differentiated teaching demand to different knowledge level of students. Because student preferences may vary by age, cultural, background, degree types, learning style and matter etc. factors to decide whether whose students are suitable to teach by either online distance learning method between individual student and whose computer or face to face learning method between students and the lecturer in classroom face to face oral teaching educational method. In fact, working adults remain strongly associated eith interest in online delivery. However, the availability of evening/weekend choices is the second most important enrollment factor to adult students, due to who consider when enrolling in an institution to indicate the important of face-to-face traditional delivery at not convenient times. So, online education is most clearly suited to independent learners those individuals who are self-motivated and self reliant and those who have a problem solving orientation.

The 2006 year Eduventures survey found that students interested in associate, bachelor's and master's degrees were most open to whole online delivery, although who were also open to campus-based delivery. Similarly, Gartner's 2008 year e-learning survey found that complete graduate programs offered online continue online. For example, international student demand for Australian higher education is expected to exceed supply in 2020 year, and key 2025 year there will be a shortfall of 22,692 international places on projected demand of 290,848. There numbers imply that to meet demand, Australian universities may want to invest further in online degree/delivery options. However, recent statistics indicate dealing interest in fully online programs in South East Asia, and a survey of 469 transnational students in 2007 year found that a majority of students opposed online provision. These findings suggest that, when branch campuses are found to be prohibitively expensive, the future of transnational programs is in programs that include face-to-face interaction facilitated by an offshore partner of the educational provider. However, education consumers prefer to combine online delivery and geographical proximity. Some of students who are living close to university campus. So who can access to courses delivered in a traditional mode, but chose to take online courses for the flexibility to it afforded them. This is an increasing trend in U.S. institutions as well, whereas online courses are used to cater solely to non-traditional students at a long distance from the campus, increasingly such classes are made available to the mainstream student constituency.

Whether online and hybrid courses will influence to university students to choose the university to study.

How can the technology online teaching contributing improve student outcome? At least, learning outcomes for students in online and hybrid courses match those of students in traditional settings. When these are reasons to believe that the hybrid model would produce more effective learning outcomes than the fully-online model in theory. Also evidence suggests that e-learning continues to grow in popularity with the number of hybrid or blended courses increasing at the fastest rate, although online/hybrid courses certainly do not outcomes courses presented the traditional (i.e. face-to-face traditional classroom) delivery method. These facts help to demonstrate that despite the popularity and increased availability of online courses. However, students still value traditional classroom methods and that online options may not significantly detract from on-campus enrollments.

Hybrid degree programs, also known as blended programs are courses of study that combine traditional classroom based instruction with significant amounts of online instruction, with each passing semester, hybrid degree programs become increasingly popular for students and universities alike. Such courses allow students to reduce time-consuming trips to campus when still benefiting from face-to-face teaching method allow colleges and universities to more effectively use classroom space and to reduce cost. For these reasons, hybrid courses are often praised as the best of both classroom and online teaching methods, it is possible that students have chance to go to classroom to listen lecturer's teaching and who also have chance to use internet to learn from online teaching method as the same time. These is no standard model for hybrid education. Some programs may have students split their time evenly between online and on-campus instruction; some may have students complete the majority of their work online with occasional intensive weekends of on-campus activity and some require students to enroll in a combination of traditional classes as well as strictly online classes. Nowadays, a major educational consulting group found that hybrid or blended learning was the most rapidly growing delivery option when online, hybrid and traditional delivery options were taken into acount. Because of the trend towards more hybrid programming, university officials concern on their potential impact on enrollment levels for on-campus degree programs. Some speculate that hybrid programs have the potential to overtake traditional programs, when others hope to use hybrid programs as stepping stones to attract more students to campus on a full time basis. The structures of different programs reflect institutions' intent to use hybrid programs to attract students from non-traditional areas. For example, Michigam State university's Master of social work hybrid program accepts roughly 25 students per year. In 2008 year, these students lived anywhere from 85 to 435 miles from the main campus, therefore frequent in person activities were not feasible. Gather in addition to completing online assignments, students attended a one-week-summer institute on campus in June and face-to-face instruction sessions in smaller groups organized by geography once per month during the fall and spring semesters. In short, hybrid programs do not necessarily replace on-campus offerings, nor do they commonly draw more students to campus on a full time basis. Rather, they complement existing program offerings by reaching out to new packets of students who have the mean to visit campus on occasion but not regularly.

In conclusion, any university ought follow its subjects, student age, school location and tuition, lecturers' repuation and school research facilities etc. factors to decide whether the course is suitable to be chose either online teaching or face-to-face traditional classroom teaching or hybrid (online and face-to-face both) teaching method to teach whose different degree level students. Because these factors will influence who to choose which kind of subjects to study. For example, if many first year students feel the subjects are difficult to learn. It implies that online distance teaching or hybrid teaching method is not suitable to be taught to them. The traditional face-to-face contact traditional classroom teaching method is more suitable to be taught to them. So, it is flexible to any one of these teaching method to choose to teach any subjects to university student. It is no absolute suitable teaching method to teach any one of subject in any one of university. Because any university is independent, it means that the teaching method is suitable to be taught to the students in the university. It doesn't mean that the same teaching method is suitable to be taught to the students to another university because every university's lecturer's reputation, school tuition fee, course's contents and qualities and student age segment and location is different among of them. It is very difficult to ensure which kind of teaching method must be suitable to be taught to the subject to all universities in any countries. Thus, if the university can predict which student individual psychology needs, then it can reduce its student turnover number successfully.

In conclusion, in behavioral economy view point, consumer decision making has long been of interest to research.

Such as this university student choice factor, e.g. university location, course design etc. factors can influence students to choose which university to study. The most prevalent model from this perspective is " utility theory" which proposes that consumers make choices based on the expected outcomes of their decisions. Some consumption psychologists view consumers are as rational decision makers and who are only concerned with self interest. However, utility theory views the consumer as a rational economic man. Consumer behavior considers a wide range of factors how to influence to change the consumer behavior , and acknowledges a board range of consumption activities beyond purchasing.

These activities commonly include need recognition, information search, evaluation of alternatives, the building of purchasing intention, the act of purchasing, consumption and final disposal. Some psychologists regard man and rational and self interested, making decisions based upon the ability to maximize utility when spending the minimum effort.

It concerns economic man theory, in order to behavior rationally in the economic sense, as consumers must aware of all the available consumption options be capable of correctly rating each alternative and be available to select the optimum course of action. Some psychologists view point, behavior is subject to biological influence through instinctive force or drives with act outside of conscious thought. So, the consumption psychological behavior is determined by biological drives, rather than individual cognition, or environmental stimuli thoughts and feelings can be regarded as consumer behaviors.

Some psychologists feel environmental variables influence consumer behaviors. However, an influential role of the environment and social experience is acknowledged with consumers activity seeking and receiving environmental and stimuli is as informational inputs aiding internal decision making . Input variables are the environmental stimuli that consumer is subjected to influence to choose either to buy or not buy the product, e.g. brand, advertisement, price, sale channel, place, salespeople service, quality, loyalty, durability etc. different elements can influence consumer final decision making.

Some investigations indicated about the changes in consumer behavior are caused by external environment influences, e.g. globalization and development of information technologies. It can help to understand the specific factors what should be taken into account in evaluation of consumer behavior.

In macroeconomic environment view point, for example, the global trend of economic liberalization, new political geography, gradual removal of international trade barriers , rapid technological advancement these environmental factors are just a few of the factors that have had major effect on the business management practices nowadays. The most obvious impact on the practical level of doing business has these macroeconomic environmental factors intensified competition. So, these factors can influence micro economical consumer behavior indirectly. Consumer behavior is mix of elements from psychology, sociology, sociopsychology, anthropology and economic. Management process will identifies, anticipates and supplies customer requirement efficiently and profitably.

In consumption psychological view point, technical criteria concerns the cost aspects of purchase, durability, reliability, comfort and convenience. Economic criteria concerns the cost aspects of purchase, include price, running costs and residual values, e.g. a trade in value of a car.

In conclusion, economic environmental and consumption psychological factors can influence consumer behavior changing, so businessmen can attempt to do any surveys, experiment etc. research methods to predict how consumer behavior will change to attract them to choose to buy their products more easily.

6.3 How to predict passenger individual consumption choice for airline industry

How can airline gas or oil price influence passenger individual airline choice?

For airline industry, if the airline firm can predict global economy trend how to influence oil or gas price, then it can predict its passenger consumption of choice more easily. Due to we are entering globalization. In Special, airline transportation demands are also increasing, due to many travelers need to catch planes to travel as well as many cargoes need to be carried to planes to transport to different countries to sell. It seems aviation transportation industry is important to influence the health of the global economy growth nowadays. However, ignorance of internal or external market dynamics, catching travelers business can be detrimental to airline profitability more than carrying cargoes business. Because the demands of travelling different countries' travelers' consumption are still more than the demands of businessmen carrying cargoes in any countries every year. So, the passenger income sector is still have the important position to compare to cargo income sector in global airline transportation industry any countries nowadays.

How can negative social change influence any airlines' air ticket prices to be risen to influence cost raising? In fact, the increase in petroleum price can have chance to affect airlines in a negative manner because increased oil prices have resulted in the reduction of services operations, the number of airline schedules flights, even airline bankruptcies. Whether inflation, terrorism, oil price, bank interest rate etc. external factors have the most influential to cause the bad effects to cause airlines need to raise air ticket price to influence traveler numbers to be decreased.

To support this hypotheses, these are my research questions, such as : Does a combination of terrorism and price of petroleum significantly influence airline profit changing mostly? The alternative hypothesis was whether a significant relationship exists between terrorism, price of petroleum and airline profitability more than other factors, such as inflation, bank interest rate of these factors cause to ticket price raising. I shall indicate that the first assumption was that terrorism has a negative effect on airline profitability and another assumption was that only external factors as oil prices or terrorism affect airline profitability.

What is the relationship of oil price and terrorism to airline industry to influence ticket price increasing?

However the effects of oil price and terrorism on airline profitability was limited to a regional perspective, e.g. the terrorism attack of plane crash event to USA on 11 Sept. After the terrorism attack happened on USA 11 Sept. incident of terrorism attack was restricted to events of skyjacking, attacks on oil production, refinery and distribution. Other types of terrorist activities, such as attacks on financial targets or senior government officials could have an adverse effect on the petroleum and airline industry. I think the disruption of the production or distribution of petroleum because of incidents of terrorism was costly in terms of loss of business and the inflationary effect on fuel dependent products or services.

In fact, some airlines have adopted more fuel saving technology, so whose fuel consumption would not use more than other non fuel saving technology airlines, these own fuel saving technology airlines which do not need to increase ticket prices to influence passenger numbers to be decreased in possible. It seems fuel price increasing will not be the only factor to influence the airline industry's traveler numbers decreasing, in addition to terrorism external incident factor influence. However, due to some airlines which have fuel saving technology, so which can avoid to use more fuel to provide planes to use and which fuel costs will be reduced, then which can provide cheaper air ticket fare prices to compare the non fuel saving technology airlines. The result will cause some airlines will lose travelling customers in this global airline travelling market, also the non fuel saving technology airlines need to renew their fuel technology if which want to keep their competitive abilities to avoid to close down their businesses.

Also, I shall indicate the financial risk of airline industry evidence from Cathay Pacific airways and China airlines against key determinants of which include interest rate, exchange rate and fuel price risk for the period of January 1996 year to December 2011 year. During this period, these key external factors which were the most serious influence to cause these two airlines choose to change their strategic behaviors. Due to any these financial risks is difficult to predict and it was also changing often, these factors will also affect any airlines stock returns which arise from changing economic conditions, e.g. fuel price movements and fluctuations in exchange rates. These external unpredicted changing factors will attribute to the air tickets cyclical demand, capital investment, fixed costs of labor and landing rights to this global airline industry.

However, the relationship between fuel price and stock prices varies across economies. The effects of oil price changes in sub-sector indices, such as wood, paper and printing, insurance and electricity. In the past, on global stock exchange market was positively significant in 2011 year. Otherwise, with respect to the U.S.A. aviation industry, some economists suggested that global airlines stock returns were negatively to percentage change in fuel prices related to any airline firm value, e.g. Qantas and Air New Zealand were negatively share price growth to fuel price risk in the short term in the 2011 year. Thus, airline industy needs to concern whether the effects of oil price changes in sub-sector indices, such as wood, paper and printing, insurance and electricity influences to predict when oil price will increase or decrease because it will lead to influence its passenger travelling numbers indirectly and these sub-sector industries have close relationship to bring cause and effect influence to oil price to airline industry.

How can demand be caused by e-service transaction channel to predict passenger individual consumption choice for airline industry?

Electronic airline ticket shopping is one good example for passengers' consumption behavioral influence. In the past, if somebody wanted to buy a book, on little learned about from whose friends or relatives, first who had to go into more bookstores to see of that book exists and after to make some price comparisons in order to decide from where to buy it from one bookstore choice only. These activities were time and money consuming. The situation has changed how the person can learn about launching a book easily from social networks, and by simply accessing an online store, such as Amazon . com , readers who can purchase the book to save time and energy by pressing a button activity only. So, the process of buying a product simplified in terms of time and money spent, but because more difficult in terms of decision making which has become more complex. The main reason is people have too many options to choose from in terms of product or service, price, quality and time.

Can digital internet technological electronic service influence consumers to choose this shopping style when who is habit to spend time to play internet . Is lifestyle a tool for understanding buyer behavior? Consumption psychologists had examined to confirm that it has relationship between the consumers' general life styles and their consumption pattern and the brands of products are used by them. They concluded that consumers often choose products, service and others because who are associated with a certain lifestyle . The products are the building blocks of lifestyle, marketers should therefore, have a complete idea of these changing lifestyles. So, dividing to segment them and position their products successfully.

The lifestyle of individuals has always been of great interest to marketers. They deal with everyday behaviorally oriented facets of people as well as their feelings, attitudes, interests and opinions. A lifestyle marketing perspective recognize that people sort themselves into groups on the basis of the things groups on the basis of the things who like to do, how who like to spend their leisure time and how who choose to spend their disposable income. Lifestyle is an important concept used in segmenting markets and understanding target customers, which is not provided by the study of demographics alone.

Many researchers have focused on identifying the lifestyle of the consumers to have better information about them. This study used the lifestyle analysis to identify market segments. Otherwise, some consumption psychologists believe to apply life style analysis for market segmentation, the developed of product strategy and the developed of the most appropriate communication strategy. They suggested successful retailers based on general application of lifestyle analysis have begun to implement a portfolio management approach which focuses on the needs of the key target markets. So, lifestyle segmentation can provide a valuable insight into the task of creating an effective brand identity. The study of lifestyle often provides fresh insights into the market and gives a more dimensional view of the target consumers. The marketing managers may be able to develop improved multi-dimensional views of key market segments, uncover new product opportunities obtain better product position, develop improved advertising communications based on a richer more life-like portrait of the target consumer and generally improve overall marketing strategy. These consumption psychologists assume that the members of any target client groups are all similar. The first hypothesis is people differ in their lifestyle they can be grouped into segments and the second hypothesis is people belonging to lifestyle segments differ in their demographics.

Thus, such as airline ticket every consumer who can either choose to buy electronic airline ticket from internet or airline shop. In travel consumption environment, a travel consumer chooses a travel agent package or a airline brand , which indicates a maximum possibility of the definition of whose lifestyle identity. Alternatively, a travelling person makes a choice in a travel consumption environment in order to define actualize whose lifestyle identity if through the travel agent package products or airline brands chosen. It can be assumed that the travelling individual's consumption behavior can be predicted from an understanding of how who represents whose would be himself/herself of the details of choosing lifestyle system are known from internet survey or questionnaire method. Thus, digital internet is one good channel to research travel consumer lifestyle to predict whose consumption style.

In economic view point, demand is a model of travel consumer behavior. It attempts to identify the factors that influence the choices that are made by travel consumers. In microeconomics, the objective of the travel consumer is to maximize the utility that can be derive given their travel choice preferences, income, the airline ticket prices relates travel package products and services for which the travel demand function in derived.

Utility is the capacity of a travel package product or service to satisfy a traveller' want. It can explain the phenomenon of travelling value. Since utility is subjective and can't be observed and measured directly. The objective in microeconomics is to maximize the satisfaction or utility of traveller individuals given their travel package preferences, incomes and the airline ticket prices of travel package products or services who buy or consume in travel market. Thus, total travel utility of more or less travel satisfaction degree be caused by traveller consumer behavior. It is the traveller consumption psychological result (effect) and it has close relationship with travel agent service.

Are internet delivered electronic services being made available to travel consumers about how who are evaluated for travel airline potential adoption to predict travel consumer behavior? Some psychologists' past researches had focused primary on the positive travel utility gains attributable to information technology adoption. However, their results indicate that e-service is adversely affect primary be performance-based risk perceptions, when perceived ease of use of the e-service reduces risk perceptions. E-services are interactive software based information systems received via internet. E-services are important in travel agent/airline e-ticket business to consumer (B2C) e airline ticket-commerce because which represent ways to provide on travel demand solutions and improving travel customer satisfaction. So, it brings this question shows that whether travel agent/airline businessmen can predict travel consumer adoption of e-services.

It is important to distinguish the different between conducting basic travel e-ticket purchase transactions and adopting e-service. The travel ticket e-service adoption decision is essentially different from most typical travel ticket e-commerce purchases as which create a longer-term relationship between the travel consumer and travel service provider. Hence, even, if travel ticket e-services are an e-commerce application to which some adoption models exists. It requires a distinct conceptualization to travel e-ticket businessmen and traditional travel agent businessmen need focuses on the role of perceived risk on influencing on adopting intentions of travel ticket e-services. When travel ticket e-services are convenient and create efficiencies for travel ticket e-businessmen users. Little is understand about how travel consumers evaluate them for adoption. So, travel ticket e-service performance quality and the potential utility of the travel service usefulness is a difficult task for travel consumers, especially given the newness of the online e-ticket visa card payment environment. If the travel consumer feels e-transaction is not suitable to him/her to use for airline ticket shopping, then it is possible that it will reduce the chance to the travel consumer to choose to use the kind of e-transaction service to buy the airline brand of travel package products.

So, this travel e-service transaction will include both risks (potential negotiations utility) and perceived usefulness (potential positive utility) to let every travel customer to feel either of high utility or low utility after who choose to use e-service to buy airline ticket shopping.

How important are risk perceptions to the overall travel e-services adoption decision? What types of risk are influenced and therefore important to the travel customer of e-service? Perceived risk is commonly thought of as an uncertainty regarding possible negative consequences of using a travel package product or service. It has formally been defined as " a combination of uncertainty plus service of outcome involved" (Bauer 1960, 1967) and " the expectation of losses associates with purchase and acts as an inhibitor to purchase behavior" (Peter & Ryam 1976). Their research's pilot test result have indicated some electronic service shoppers, such as airline e-ticket buyers concern for the theft of their private information, or simply its misuse by the travel businessmen collecting it. Members of a focus group drawn from the population studied to concern for the loss of privacy of personal financial information as an identify-theft. So, privacy risk was gathered and modeled as a deterrent to utility evaluations and the adoption choice to influence consumers choices to buy the product from this e-service sale channel.

Overall, some consumers will feel those perceived risks to influence who decide to buy the travel ticket package product from e-service sale channel. Such as performance risk, it means the possibility of the product manufacturing and not performing as it was designed and advertised and failing to deliver the desired benefits, financial risk, it means the potential monetary outlet associated with the initial purchase price as well as the subsequent maintenance cost of the travel package product (ibid). The current financial services include potential for financial loss , due to fraud, time with means travel consumers may lose time when making a bad purchasing decision by wasting time researching and making the purchased, learning ow to use a product or service only to have to replace if it does not perform to expectations, psychological risk means potential loss of self oneself. Travel consumers feel unwise if they experience a non-performing travel package products and may experience their feelings of harm to their self-image from the frustration of not achieve their buying goals, social risk means potential loss of status in one's social group as a result of adopting a travel package product or service, looking foolish, privacy risk means potential loss of control over personal information, such as when information about travel package purchase used without the travel customer's knowledge or permission. A travel consumer is carrying a criminal use whose identity to perform fraudulent transactions. Overall , when any one consumer feels one of those perceived risk will occur, then any one of these risks will influence who to choose to use e-service transactions method to buy travel package product from internet. So, travel package internet shopping seems have bad image to influence travel consumer shopping choice of channel as well as travel consumer demand of the travel package product will be reduced if who feel e-ticekt service transaction channel is not safe to whom.

Is online video and television service is to be affective in predicting technology adoption to influence consumption behavior choice? It seems online video and television and online e-ticket travel package service which are similar to behavioral economy analysis. Such as the online entertainment consumer who can use computer to watch online video and television in anywhere, e.g. library, at home etc. places. Even some online video and television service can provide free charge to let any entertainment consumer to watch any time from internet. So, who will feel no any expense. Online e-ticket buying service can let the travel consumer use whose computer to compare any airline companies' e-tickets prices and travel date and time schedule and travel destination from internet at home conveniently. So, who does not need to spend transportation cost or driver whose car to to to the travel agent or airline to buy paper airline ticket. Hence, both online video and television rent service and e-airline ticket consumption services can help consumers spend less time and expense to make consumption decision at home in short time. It is a popular online consumption behavioral economy model.

Nowadays, online video and television services have become one of the most promising activities in terms of advertising revenue. E-Marketer has estimated that online video or television advertising will soar at 56% to 70% in the next five years (Halleman, 2008). To predict user acceptance of online video and television services. Despite a digital growth in online video and television to service over the span of a few years.

What factors can influence consumers to choose to buy the product after who watch online video and television advertising? Some psychological experiments shows a greater influence of perceived behavioral control on intention to use this type of services. The effects of attitude toward use and subjective norm were positive, but more moderate. The lesser effect of attitude towards use may be explained by the evidence benefits of watching videos online. However, search recent consumer studies have confirmed that watching online videos and televisions has become one of the favorite online activities for internet users (Hallerman 2008. Mulligan et al. 2008).

Hence, airline ticket consumer individual behavior can apply e-service questionnaires survey channel to gather what who needs or expectation are chosen to buy any prefer airlines to predict how to satisfy or attract whom final travel consumption of decision more easily.

Can advertising influence consumption behavior?

Advertising is a subject on which people tend to hold strong and often opposing views, and economists are not expectations to this. Some economists regard advertising as one means by which firms concentrate on promoting whose tastes and opinions in the direction of their products and also more generally in favor of private consumption (consumer behavior). Other economists see advertising as an efficient way by which firms supply information to potential consumers. Otherwise, some economists see advertising as a barrier inhibiting new entrants into an industry thereby enabling the established firms to reap high profits, when others see advertising as evidence of competition and an aid to new entrants in establishing themselves. So, it seems advertising can influence consumer choices possibly.

Advertising relatives to sales varies considerably between industries. For example, the ratio of advertising in 1968 year varied from over 15% in the toilet preparations industry to over 10% in the soap and detergents industry to near is in a number of toilet preparation producer industries. A distinction is frequently made between information an persuasive advertising , and it is often suggested that some forms of advertising (such as classified ads.) are likely to have more informative content than other forms (such as television advertising).

What is the sale of advertising in the demand function? One response is that a firm can sell more of its products because consumers have more information on that product. The information may relate to its existence, price, quality etc. Thus advertising is seen as essentially supplying information to consumers how to choose the similar kinds of products to decide which is the suitable product to buy. The other response is that advertising seeks to persuade consumers to purchase with favored people or situations, repetition of the same message. This advertising seeks to promote tastes rather than to inform. One firms' advertising may not be successful through false judgement by that firm and its advertisers or because of the impact of the advertising of other firms. The difference between the two responses can be put in terms of the conventional; utility maximization approach top consumer demand theory. The first response regards consumers' taste (i.e. the utility function) as fixed and advertising informs the consumer about availability, price etc. So, that utility maximizing process can take place more effectively . The second response regards advertising and seeking to promote consumers' tastes and change the consumers' utility function in a manner favorable to the advertiser. So, different types of advertising have been as containing information and persuasion in varying proportions and varying in the degree of desirability. But for the firm, the intention is to sell its products, and it will present any information in a way which seeks to influence the consumer to purchase its products.

Some consumption psychologists believe utility maximization by well-informed individuals plays a central role in conventional micro-economies. However, advertising can be a part of the conduct of firms in that firms use advertising amongst many other things to seek to increase profits or whatever their objectives it. Finally, advertising can be a part of performance, influenced by industrial structure. Some consumption psychologists also believe the highly differentiated products are more suitable for advertising than undifferentiated ones. They suppose existing firms benefit from their past investment in advertising and new entrants have to overcome those advantage.

If advertising is a profitable activity for firms to undertake, then the question arises as to why other firms don't follow suit. If other firms possibly including new entrants did follow suit, then the returns to advertising are likely to be reduced. It is useful to discuss the returns to advertising in terms of the returns in increased sales per advertising message and the cost of delivering an advertising message. Increasing return would occur form a message of repeated showing of a particular advertisement led to the product demand increasing at an increasing rate. Thus, of the product demand per unit of time is same to the number of advertising message per unit of time, then increasing sale returns would be raised possibly. The implications of any increasing sale returns to advertising may depend upon whether the increasing returns operate for advertising of a single product or for advertising of a number of products. Thus, it seems advertising promotion behavior can create barriers to entry to reduce consumers have more choices from other competitors' similar products sale. Such as any airline businesses can attempt to use advertising to attract travellers to concern what they can give different or unique or excellent airline service to let travellers feel which airline service is more especial to compare other airline competitors, during external environment factor influence consumer travel desire , such as fuel rising or unemployment etc. external poor environment factor influence to global airline travel market. Hence, airline advertising promotion method can let travellers to feel why (what reasons) who ought to find the airline travelling service.

How can airline atmosphere environment influence traveller travel choice behavior?

On the one hand, some consumption psychologists suggest in-store variable factor can influence consumer emotion to feel either pleasure or displeasure of intended shopping behaviors within the store, thus these consumption psychologists who believe retail store environment can influence consumption behavior. On the other hand, some employment psychologists also suggest work environment can influence employee individual emotion to work, work environment include hospitals, schools and prisons etc. public work environment. It seems consumers and employees whose emotion will be influenced by environment factor. It brings this question. Can store atmosphere environment predict consumers buying decision?

These consumption psychologists feel the component of store image, physical in-store variable , such as aisle width, brightness and crowding, when clearly these physical variables are store environment's major factor which can influence consumption behavior will be changed. Some retailers have claimed large effects from manipulating store atmosphere via layout, lighting, color and music (Wysocki 1979; Stevens 1980).

Some consumption psychologists also show these avoidance behaviors can cause consumer individual shopping emotion. First, physical approach and avoidance, which can be related to store patronage intentions at a basic level. Exploratory approach and avoidance can be related to in-store search and exposure to a broad or narrow range of retail offerings. Second, Communication approach and avoidance can be related to interaction with sales personnel and floor staff. Third, performance and satisfaction approach and avoidance can be related to repeat shopping frequency as well as reinforcement of time and money expenditures in the store.

In consumer psychological view point, pleasure or displeasure refers to the degree to which the consumer feels good, joyful, happy or satisfied in the situation. Then, another degree to which a consumer feels excited, stimulated, alert or active in the situation. Thus, if the consumer feels the shopping environment is comfortable, joyful, happy or satisfied. The shopping environment, it will have more chance to influence the consumer chooses shopping. Otherwise if, the consumer feels the shopping environment is excited, alert, stimulated or active. The shopping environment will have less chance to influence the consumer chooses shopping. It seems each consumer individual emotion will influence whose consumption behavior as well as store atmosphere environment has close relationship to influence each consumer individual emotion also.

Thus, retailers need to concern how to design whose store environment, e.g. what kind of furniture color, style and size; how much area of the store. For example, the store area is either large or middle or small area to let many or small number of consumers to stay in the store at the same time. How to let consumers to enter or leave the store? For example, how to let consumers to feel to leave the store easily when the fire is happening in store, it can make the consumers feel more safe, so who will have more probable to stay in the store to consume. How to display whose products to let consumers feel to touch or see to find any products on the shelves more easily. Choosing what kind of music to let consumers to listen during who are staying to shopping in store, e.g. soft music or none any music (quiet environment). These different store external feeling factors will influence each consumer individual emotion to feel more comfortable or uncomfortable feeling to decide to spend more long time or short time to stay in the store. Thus, it seems store atmosphere environment can influence consumer individual shopping behavior, so retailers can not neglect how to design store atmosphere environment to let whose customers feel more comfortable and safe to stay in stores.

Hence, it seems that if any airline company which can design attractive service counter environment to let travellers feel the airline service counter comfortable and enjoyable. It will have possible to influence them to choose to buy any travel package service from the attractive airline atmosphere environment influence more easily. So, atmosphere environment has indirect factor to influence consumer to consume more easily.

How can airline counter servicer knowledge influence traveller consumption behavior?

Can model for understanding service encounter evaluation that can synthesize consumer satisfaction, services marketing, and attribution to influence consumption behavior to the retailer? Can airline servicer travel knowledge and service attitude influence traveller consumption of decison making ? These factors concern on the service industries how to influence consumption behavior, which focus on service encounter satisfaction and service quality to both the importance and the complexity of the issues. First and foremost, customer satisfaction depends directly and most immediately on the management and monitoring of individual service encounters (Parasuraman, Zeithaml, and Berry 1985; Shostack 1984, 1987; Sollmon et al. 1985).

What is the conceptual definition of service encounter? The model of service encounter evaluation relies on Shostack's (1985, p.243) definition of the term" service encounter" as " a period of time during which a consumer directly interacts with a service." The author identified all aspects of the service firm with which the consumer may interact, including its personnel, its physical facilities and other tangible elements, during a given period of time. I give this hypothesis, such as when an employee offers to compensate the customer for service failure, the offer may influence attributions. The employee performance will lead the customer to have negative beliefs about the firm, when the bad employee offer leads the customer to think bad image to the firm. So, the employee's bad service attitude can influence the offer is made to compensate for service failure to build bad service image to the company. Moreover, physical surroundings also are hypothesized to influence customer emotion in service failure situations. For example, if a customer experiences service failure in an organized , professional environment, e.g. lawyer, doctor, accountant professional services. The customer may not have more confidence to find the firm to serve to him again. In contrast, in a disorganized environment, the physical cues may suggest incompetence, inefficiency and poor service. In such an environment, the customer may attribute greater responsibility to the firm and be more likely to expect the same type of problem to occur in the future. Thus, any professional service firms, whose employees' service performance can influence customers' confidence to decide to find whose professionals to give any professional service opinions again. Thus, any professional service firm, whose employees' service performance can influence customers' confidence to the service firm likely.

How can the impact of personality and emotion on post-purchase service processes influence consumption behavior? Will consumption behavior be influenced to the retailer by consumer satisfaction or dissatisfaction and post-purchase service behaviors? Such as complaints, recommendations, and repeat purchase intentions, toward loyalty and word of mouth. Developing a new customer is expensive. Particularly in mature markets, competition is strong, product differentiation is low, and promotional costs have skyrocketed. So, understanding who these customers are, why who are dissatisfied, and how or even whether to market to them is an increasingly important issue.

That a customer's level of satisfaction affects much post-purchase behaviors, such as complaining and negative word of mouth is well documented. Satisfaction itself is influenced by comparing actual product performance to expectation. So, some consumption actual product performance will be needed to expectations by the product manufacuter or seller. So, some consumption psychologists began to research that the role of consumption based emotion in consumer satisfaction formation how to make recent personality research particularly concerning. It seems post-purchase processed can be a response to influence consumption- based emotions and consumption behavior to any retailers. The degree of satisfaction is a specific consumption experience, it has a direct impact on such post-purchase processes as repeat purchase intentions and complaining. So, any retailers need to concern on how predicting post-purchase consumer behavior will be.

Because personality should be an important predictor of consumption experiences, and thereby of post-purchase processes. Post-purchase processes can include either on positive consumption-based emotions or on negative consumption-based emotions. When the consumer satisfies to use the product, the useful of product expectation will be increased. Otherwise, when the consumer dissatisfies to use the product, the useful of product expectation will be decreased and the consumer complaint behavior will be increased. So, it seems post-purchase processes can influence consumers to decide to continue to choose to buy the products from the retailer again as well as how to reduce consumers have negative emotions to the products which is an important factor to influence any consumption behavior changing to the retailer. Hence, airline or travel agent counter servicer's attitude and travel knowledge will have either positive or negative influence to any traveller's final travel decision.

In -store consumer digital signage behavior how can influence consumer behavior

Digital signage is a new technology, where people broadcasting displays adapt their content to the audience demographic and features. In some shopping centers, retailers like to use machine learning methods on real-world digital signage viewer data to predict consumer behavior in a retail environment. Digital signage systems are nowadays primarily used as public information interfaces. They display general information, advertise content or serve as media for enhanced customer experience.

Interaction design studies show that the interaction level of users with digital signage systems will increase, including also the mobility of users around the display. Since digital signage systems can have a significant effect on commerce, which are also rapidly shopping centers ad retail stores. Retail generalization studies reveal that in-store digital signage increases customer traffic and sales (Burke, 2009).

Some consumer psychologists believe purchase decision processes can be described with five stages. The first stage is problem recognition, where consumer recognizes a problem is a need. The second stage is search for information via heightened attention of consumer towards information about a certain product, which can even resolve in actual proactive search for information. The third stage represents the evaluation of alternatives , which usually involves a comparison between various options and features based in the models of the expected value and beliefs. In the fourth stage of the purchase decision process, a provider, place, time, value , type and quality of the selected product or service and determined. The fifth stage are the final stage describes the post purchase use, behavior and actions.

Why will digital signage influence consumers choose to buy the product? It is possible that some consumers who like to use visa card to go to shopping as well as who like to use digital signage to confirm who are the visa card holders to let the businessmen to feel who are rich to let bank give trust to issue visa card to them to use. So, who do not need to bring much money to leave home to prepare to buy anything and who only bring one visa card to leave home safely. Thus, the digital signage systems are a new approach to automatic modelling of in-store consumer behavior based on audience measurement data. It is a unique machine payment method, which can also be used to predict more distinctive characteristics, such as an consumer individual's role in the purchase decision process. So, I believe digital signage audience measurement data can be used to model various user behavior for one kind of in-store consumer behavior prediction of method. Hence, it seems travel agent or airline can choose to apply visa card signature method to encourage travellers to make travel package purchase decision more easily by this electronic card payment method.

6.4 How does MTR (Mass Train Railway) need to
consider route design location of choice?

Introduction

Nowadays, transportation and economic development have close relationship. Economic development stimulates transportation demand by increasing the numbers of workers commuting to and from work, customers traveling to and from services areas, and products being moving by lorries on the roads between products and customers. According to Bailey, Mokhtarian and Little (2008) indicated "transportation route is past of distinct development pattern or road network and mostly described by regular street patterns as an important factor of human existence, development and civilization. The route network combined with increased road transportation investment result in changed levels of conveniently reflected through cost benefit analysis, savings in travel time, and other benefits. " These benefits are noticeable in increased catchment areas for services and facilities , shops, schools, offices, banks and leisure activities by transportation route design of location choice.

Why MTR underground train transportation needs to know passenger behaviour

Understanding individual passenger behaviour is essential for the design MTR transportation, because who can choose to catch bus, taxi, tram, train ferry etc. different kinds of public transportation tools. Individual traveler who decides to catch which kinds of public transportation tools, it depends on whether the public transportation tool can provide real time travel information, liking link travel time schedule. So, any country's (MTR) mass transit railway transportation enterprises need to understand where it has terminal to give convenience to the local living areas of time travelers to choose to catch MTR easily. Although, MTR ticket fare is one factor to influence any passengers choice. But, those other factors can also influence them to choice. e.g. MTR any terminal location of convenience, short time travelling, none crowding in busy (peak) time, MTR platform waiting arrival time, none sudden MTR engineering machines broken accident events occurrence frequently etc. different factors, any one of these factors which can influence passengers who choose to catch MTR or other kinds of transportation tools.

Why route choice can influence passenger behavioural choice
Usually, the busy time passengers will regard the route choice as a coordination problem to influence them to choose to catch which kinds of transportation tools. The route choice is as an opportunity costs to influence any busy time passengers to decide to choose to catch which kind of transportation tool which is the best right choice in the right time among of them. In the short time, for example, it seems any busy time passengers will choose to catch bus to substitute MTR underground train transportation tool, due to who feels the bus can arrive any destinations to compare other kinds of transportation tools in the most short time. However even if the MTR can either charge cheaper ticket fare to sell full day or charge discount ticket fare to sell in the busy (peak) time to compare to bus fare. It is possible that the busy time passengers will still choose to catch bus, if between the bus terminal and the another bus terminal that distance is the shorter time route to spend time to arrive destination to compare between the MTR terminal to the another MTR terminal arrival time . Also, although the busy time passengers will feel to enounter traffic jam to influence sitting or waiting bus time to be longer time in possible and who also feel MTR can avoid traffic jam problem. However, usually any busy (peak) time passengers will feel the chance of traffic jam occurrence will be less. So, the short bus route choice is more potential factor to influence the busy (peak) time passengers still to choose bus to catch.

However, if anyone wants to investigate results of day-to-day route choice which can be transferred to more realistic environment. It is necessary to explore individual behaviour in an interactive experimental set up to ensure busy (peak) time passenger transportation behavioural choice. For example, a passenger has a choice between a main road (M) and a side road (S) for travelling from (A) to (B). (M) is faster if (M) and (S) are chose by the same number of passengers. So, this method can be researched whether MTR terminal station is located at the main road (M) or the side road (S) where is more suitable to accept to passengers generally.

Why trip time reliability and crowding factors can influence MTR passenger choice.

Other problem is MTR busy (peak) time's crowding in public transportation occurrence of MTR underground train transportation tool is becoming a growth to concern as MTR demand growth at a busy (peak) time. To capture the MTR passengers benefits with reduced crowding from improved MTR public transport service and image. It is necessary a identify the relevant dimensions of crowding that are meaningful measures of what crowding means to MTR passengers. Two main influences on MTR model choice that are growing in relevance are trip time reliability and crowding. It represents a benefit-cost framework. In fact, MTR passengers can be willing to pay more expensive ticket fare, it MTR can avoid crowding and short and the accurate arrival trip time between terminals is reliable to occur. How to measure of MTR crowding, e.g. weighting the gap between the busy time, the standard (i.e. objective) and the perceived (i.e. subjective) metrics. We are not in a position to definitely map the two dimensions, which is a crucial requirement for translating objective improvements into equivalent subjective gains that then can be applied, willingness to pay estimates MTR ticket fares to obtain the additional MTR passenger benefits of MTR public transportation investment to any terminal stations.

Because MTR crowding has a negative impact on passengers in terms of psychological on emotional distress. MTR passengers are willing to stand for up to 20 minutes of the service is fast and reliable usually. However crowding outweighed these benefits from a MTR passenger's perpective, experienced crowding leads a increased dissatisfaction. e.g. stress and less privacy during who needs to stand up in MTR. Due to there are no enough places to supply to them to stand up in MTR. If the MTR trip time was longer time between the passenger's terminals, who will feel more dissatisfaction and it will cause who feels whether who ought need to choose to catch other transportation tools to substitute MTR next time. e.g. bus, train, tram, ferry, taxi etc. So, from an operator's perspective, the MTR service frequency or MTR size is significantly influenced by the level of ridership, which sends a signal to respond if the monitored crowding level exceeds the benchmark standard in the busy time. e.g. in the morning time or at the night time, the students or employment people who need to go to schools or offices (working places). The locations of different places between MTR terminals and crowding are regarded as a key service attribute for MTR pubic transportation along with other factors, such as travelling time and reliability, e.g. service quality, none engineering machines are broken to cause MTR stops suddenly.

Given the increasing importance of crowding on both the disutility to existing MTR public transportation users and the influence to it. MTR passenger can choose to use either the MTR public public transportation or other public transportation. It is timely to review the MTR current measures of crowding defined by transportation authorities. MTR operators ought evaluate whether they apporpriately reflect MTR each traveler experiences and perceptions of crowding in busy (peak) time. I suggest that MTR needs to buy other underground trains to supply to the busy (peak) time passengers to let them have enough seats to sit down, so who do not need to stand up in any MTR underground trains when they catch MTR underground trains in busy time. It aims to let who are willingness to pay the estimation of reasonable ticket fares to compare the other kinds of transportation tools in the busy (peak) time.

How MTR can attract many passengers.

On the commuter departure time choice of any reference point researching hand, the departure time decisions of communters are of fundamental importance of peak period MTR traffic congestion. However, whether on the demand side, MTR underground train congestion relief measures, such as MTR ticket fare to every terminal station needs to be charged cheaper fare or discount fare in the peak (busy) time every day. To aim to attract many passengers to choose to catch MTR Underground train public transportation tools, substitute to choose other public transportation tools in the peak time.

Over the past decades, there have been very active research efforts in the departure time problem, both in econometric modeling and dynamic user equilibrium fields. Although, these works provide valuable insights into dynamic commuter decision making, they do not identify the commuters' response to gains and losses related to whole actual arrival time to reference points who may have relative. The appliability of the reference point hypothesis of prospect theory to the commuter's departure time decision making to obtain a better understanding of how departure time choice in MTR platform during their waiting underground train arrival time. However, every MTR underground train actual arrival time and deviation variables related to reference points (gains and losses) are the key factors in the departure time choice model. How the MTR underground train of every communter's daily departure time decision can be modelled when the reference point hypothesis of prospect theory. The MTR underground train's schedule delay is defined as the difference between the preferred arrival time (PAT) and the actual arrival time (AT) for a given MTR commuter. In a daily MTR commute, a commuter in the indifference band actual arrival time is an essential feature of MTR schedule study. Two reference points are the earliest acceptable arrival time and the work starting time for a given MTR platform waiting passengers. In psychological view point, prospect theory proposes that the displeasure of a loss is perceived or greater than the pleasure of a gain of the same attitude and therefore, the value function is stronger for losses than gains.

To conclude, it seems that if MTR waiting passengers need not spend long time to wait underground train arrival in platform and it can provide seats to let them to sit down in the busy (peak) crowding time. It will make them to feel pleasure, even the MTR ticket fare is not fair and reasonable to charge higher fare to compare other kinds of public transportation tools fares. So the peak waiting time factor can influence the passengers to choose other kind of transportation tools to catch easily. Moreover, MTR's two reference points are the earliest role. Similarly a loss is observed when the MTR platform waiting commuter experiences or actual arrival time which is beyond that the MTR schedule time. Due to that a MTR waiting commuter is as an early side arrival of whose actual arrival time is earlier than whose preferred arrival time.

In general,passenger transportation choice consumption behavior is similar to alcohol choiceconsumption behavior.Because some passengers choose to catch the kind of transportation tool , it is habit cause. Such as some alcohol consumers who oftern drive the brand of alcohol , it is habit cause also.

Some consumption psychologists had attempt to research whether planned behavior can predict alcohol consumption. This research aims to quantify variables between theory of planned behavior variables and (i) intentions to consume alcohol in habit and (ii) reducing alcohol consumption reasons. They showed some drunken violence alcohol consumers who will reduce to consume much alcohol if who feel driving accident or causing death or violence behavior or alcohol poison causing non-health after who have consumed too much alcohol often. Thus, it is important to understand the psychological determinants of alcohol consumption.

A model of human behavior that has been extensively utilized to predict health-related behaviors, such as alcohol consumption in the theory planned (TPB; Ajzen, 1991). This model proposes that the most important determinant of behavior is a person's intention to perform the behavior. Three variables are identified as determinants intention, attitude, subjective norm and perceived behavioral control . Attitudes are an individual's positive or negative evaluation of performing the behavior. Subjective norms reflect an individual's perceptions of social approach or disapproval for performing the behavior. It represents an individual's perceptions of control over behavioral performance in the face of internal and external barriers. These results suggest the possibility that alcohol consumer behavior that are harmful to health, such as alcohol consumption, may yield different relationships when compared with results for behaviors that are beneficial to health. Specifically, individuals may wish to emphasis a lack of control over health risk behaviors, because these behaviors are not seen as socially , desirable and may need to be explained away be reference to external causes, such as peer pressure (De Visser & Mc Donnell, 2013).

It seems that the passenger will reduce times to catch the kind of transportation tool if who feels the kind of transportation is dangerous (not safe) , such as if the alcohol consumer feels the alcohol will cause unhealth to him/ her. Then, who will also reduce times to choose to buy the brand of alcohol to drink.

Hence, it seems fear feeling psychological factor can influence alcohol consumers to reduce alcohol consumption in these situations, such as what action is being considered (e.g. heavy episodic drinking and the action is located (e.g. driving car) and what is the time frame for the action(e.g. needs car), the staff is a company driver when needs to drive car every day. Thus, whose action will influence to reduce whose alcohol consumption. Although, who has drinking alcohol in habit, but because who is one company driver, who is fear to cause accident to hurt himself/ herself and whose staffs when who sit in whose company car together. So, who will choose to reduce to consume alcohol in possible. Hence, dangerous is one most factor to influence passengers who do not choose to catch it.

However, social mobile analysis is a good method to research what the main factors which can influence passengers to either choose to catch MTR or choose other transportation tools, such as bus, tram, train, ferry , taxi etc. Some consumption psychologists had using a data set involving on adults (26 couples) living in a community for over a year to find that social behavior measured via face-to-face interaction, call and SMS logs, which can be used to predict the spending behavior to explore diverse business because loyal customers and overspend. Their results showed the mobile phone bases social interaction patterns can provide more predictive power on spending behavior than personality based features. Interestingly , these consumption psychologists found that more social couples also tend to overspend. Obtaining such insights about couple level spending behavior via novel social-computing frameworks can be of vital importance to economists, marketing professional and policy markers.

The basic idea is that a person's attitudes and behaviors are influenced by several levels of society, such as culture, subculture, social classes, reference groups and face-to-face groups. Such as any passenger's transportation tools choice, which are also influenced by culture, subculture, social classes, near transportation tool place, transportion cost, transportation time schedule and transportation service etc. factors.

In Special finally, some consumption psychologists investigated whether the social behavior measured via face-to-face interactions, call and SMS logs can be used to predict the spending behavior for couples in terms of their propensity to explore diverse businesses, engage frequently with them and overspend. Their findings not only motivate in potentially new line of investigation into a spending behavior via mobile sensing , but also demonstrate the feasibility of passive (i.e. which don't require active user attention) method, for undertaking similar studies at a large scale in near future.

In recent years, mobile sensing and reality approaches have been used to understand multiple aspects of human behavior. Insights on a behavioral level (e.g. overspending, loyalty and diversity) have much longer term validity and can explain certain aspects of human behavior. To study spending behavior of couples, the consumption psychologists focus on three important behavior : exploration, loyalty and overspending behavior. The aim is to identify the couples that tend to explore diverse business, engages repeatedly and frequently with certain businesses and (or) spend higher amounts of income to them. For exploration, who calculated the diversity in vendors frequented. The exact method for calculating diversity scores is explained in the next section. For loyalty, who considered how frequently couples engage with their favorite businesses. Specifically, they calculated the percentage of transactions (out of a couple's total transactions), that were made at their top businesses. Lastly, to quantify overspending, they calculated the ratio of the amount of money spent by a couple to their self-declared discretionary spending budget. Hence MTR can use mobile to enquire what are the general expectation to any passengers in order to predict the reasons why who prefer to choose other transporation tools more accurate.

How to apply online psychological advertising method to predict passenger behavioral consumption?

Online advertising can give relevance information to represent the similarity between advertisement and queries. These existing online advertisement works mainly focused on interpreting advertisements clicks in term of what consumers seek. (i.e. relevance information) and how consumers choose to watch TV or magazine or online advertisement etc. from different promotion media. (historically to know the product is selling on the market through advertising information). However, few of manufacturers or sellers attempted to understand why consumers chose to watch the advertising from TV or magazine or internet etc. different media.

Why can MTR can choose online advertisement to predict passenger behavior? Online Advertisement can be as a commercial search engine for manufacturers or sellers to gather data to concern how behavioral consumption is. The online advertisement's each observations motivate who to systemically model to test what each consumer individual psychological desire in order for a precise prediction on behavioral consumption after online advertisement promotion from internet media.

Today, internet is one kind of effective psychological advertising promotion method. For example, an online advertisement system, sponsored search has been one of the most important business models for commercial web search engines. It generates most of the revenue of search engines by presenting to users sponsored search results, i.e. advertisements (ads), along with organic search results. To deliver the most interesting ads to the users, a sponsored search system consists of technical components, including query-to-ads matching, online click prediction for matched ads, online click probability and auction to determine the ranking, placement, and pricing of the remaining ads. To aim to attempt to predict behavioral consumption for any kinds of product sale from online advertisement media.

In today's industry, generalized second price auction (GSP) is the most widely-used auction mechanism , in which the price that an advertiser has to pay depends on the predicted online click probability of the online buyers, whose own ads as well as the bid price and predicted online click probability of the ads ranked in the next position. The online sponsored search systems typically employ a machine learning model top predict the probability that an online user clicks an advertising from internet.

However, in practical sponsored search system. There are many ads without adequate historical click through data, even after query levels. Then online ads can been click improved prediction accuracy to consumer individual behavioral consumption when each click is occurred to the seller individual website. For example, online ads, such as : free Nike coupons ad. It shows " Go-Get_couptons.com/Nike, Download and print Nike coupons (100% Free)" ; another Nike-sales prices ad. It shows www.calibex.com, clothing, latest fashions and styles on sale. Buy Nike Fast!" ; another Perfume.com official site ad. It shows "www.perfume.com, 10,000 + brand name perfumes and colognes-up to 80% off retail!" ; another Luxury English Perfume Ad. It shows " www.florislondon.com, shop online for luxury perfumes for men, women and the home". Above of these are example online ads. For two queries, "Nike" and "Perfume" , and two ads under the same query field similar relevance to the query.

Despite the usefulness of the relevance and historical of what users click and how users click. Specially, relevance information can indicate what relevant content users seek to click from online (internet) media. However, as it is well-known that users are not active to search for ads., the search engine, instead has to recommend ads. To users during their generic web search. Therefore, the relevance between query and ad can't perform as the key driver for click. In my opinion, in order for more click prediction, businessmen need to examine why users click.

Thus, MTR can use online advertisement to gather any passenger opinions concerning these questions: What will influence them to choose to catch other transportation tools, instead of MTR? What are MTR passengers expectations when who are catching MTR transportation tool? etc. different consumption psychologial questions.

How to apply psychological research to analyze of online user desire in sponsored search for behavioral consumption of reasons? First, according to literatures on consumer behavioral analyses, many factors will influence the decision making for consumption, including thought based effects and feeling-based effects. Though-based effects are basically win or loss analysis (e.g. trade-off between price and quantity), when feeling-based effects are more subjective (e.g. brand loyalty and luxury seeking). Note users online clicking the ad. Usually are with the intention to purchase something. In this situation, it is natural that the factors mentioned in consumer behavior analyses will influence their online click behaviors.

So, MTR advertisers can gather online advertisement data to choose how to design whose online advertisement to follow either is based on win or loss analysis, either focusing on MTR ticket price and MTR service performance quality features or is based on more subjective analysis , focusing on MTR brand loyalty and luxury(high income passenger segment) seeking features to attract any MTR passengers individual attention to choose to watch MTR online advertisements from online advertisement media more easily. So, it seems that online advertisement is a promotional and gathering data channel to persuade MTR passenger individual attention to predict these influence factor: how to change or improve MTR service performance or MTR station location choice or how to arrange busy time and non busy time MTR ticket price etc. influence factor in order to design MTR online advertisement to attract many passengers change their attitude to prefer choose to catch MTR transporation tools.

Does habit strength moderate the intention behavior to consumption?

Scientific evidence provides a sufficiently strong basis to justify the systematic development of intervention programs to increase healthy nutrition behaviors (World Health Organization, 2003). Such as an adequate consumption of fruit, a high consumption of fruit is associated with lower risk of cancer (Kremers et al., 2005, World Health Organization, 2003).

Will the concept of habit influence consumption behavior? Such as, fruit is a kind of health food. If the consumer has habit to choose to buy different kinds of fruit to eat everyday. Is habit as a factor to influence the consumer to choose to buy fruit to eat? Otherwise, if the consumer has no habit to choose to buy different kinds of fruit to eat everyday. Is non-habit as a factor to influence the consumer individual consumption behavior to choose any kinds of fruit to eat everyday.

Traditionally, habit has been measured by the number of times that behavior has already been performed in the past by an individual. Evidence to date indicates direct effects of past behavior on current behavior (Conner & Abraham, 2001). Some consumption psychologists had done experiment to research whether habit factor can influence fruit consumption. Their showed fruit consumption was assessed with a five item questionnaire, which was validated against seven day dietary records and biomarker for fruit intake (Bogers et. al 2004).

According to this consumption questionnaire result, it showed that intention is hypothesized to be the most immediate determinant of consumption behavior, yet several recent lines of research suggest that intentional control of behavior may be difficult to change, due to habit behavior consumption is caused to the individual consumer. Thus, it is difficult to change the consumer's behavior, when who have habit to choose to consume different kinds of fruit every week. However, results showed that the influence of intention on fruit consumption was weak and non-significant for those who had a strong habit toward fruit consumption. In constant, for those with a low or medium habit strength towards fruit. For those with low/medium habit strength, path analyses confirmed the reasoned, intentional process is for fruit consumption. In contrast, for those with high habit strength, it had the strongest influence on behavior. Thus, perceived control ability of fruit consumption seems to overrule the planned and intentional processes of fruit consumption for those with a strong habit. The environment behavior link also relates to the origins of habit, which are thought to originate from repeated performance of a given behavior in a stable situation. Thus, it seems environment can be one factor to influence strong habit consumers to buy fruit to eat every week as well as strong habit fruit consumer will buy much fruit to eat more than weak habit fruit consumer per week.

Hence, MTR needs to change any passenger's transportation tool choice of habit, after the passenger's habit has been changed. Then , MTR will have more passenger numbers chance.

6.5 Why environment protection product businessmen need to concern what the degree of quality of life to their potential buyers

Why environment protection product businessmen need to concern what the degree of quality of life to their potential buyers. Because if the potential buyers felt whose quality of life is good , so who will fell air or water pollution is not serious to influence whose health. Then, who will not have more needs to choose to buy any environmental protection products. Otherwise, if the potential buyers felt whose quality of life is bad, so who will feel air and water pollution is serious to influence whose health,. Then, who will have more needs to choose to buy any environmental protecton products. Some researchers have showed that human rights to identify the factors that need to be included in a quality of life measure. But, even if accepted as a starting point, that still does not point to clear to indicators or how which are to be weighted. So, a technocratic and unsatisfying device that is sometimes used is to recort to " expert opinion". So, it implies that if the country had any environment scientists prove the country's air and water pollution is serious, then the environment scientists' opions will be possible to influence the country's citizen consider to attend to buy any environmental protection products to protect those health.

I suggest environment protection products firms can use surveys methods to enquire whose country's citizen ideas concerning their feeling of quality of life. How to use life satisfaction surveys to measure human quality of life? Some researchers had been carrying on researching a methodologically improved and more comprehensive measure of qualify of life satisfaction surveys. Surveys of life satisfaction is as opposed to surveys of the related concept of happiness, are preferred for a number of reasons, such as GDP statistic method. These surveys ask people the simple question of how satisfied who are with their lives in general. A typical question is on the four point scale used to the surveys studies. For example, on the whole are you very satisfied, fairly satisfied, not vey satisfied, or not at all satisfied with the life you lead? The results of the surveys have been attracting growing interest in recent years. Despite a range of early criticism, such as cultural non-comparability, the effect of language differences across countries, psychological factors distorting responses, tests have disproved as migitated most concerns. One objection is that responses to surveys don't adequately reflect how people really feel about their life. However, responses to questions about life satisfaction tend to be promoted, non-response rates are very low. This simple measure of life satisfaction has been found to correlate highly with more sophisticated test ratings by others who know the individual, and behavioral measures. The survey results have on the whole proved far more reliable and information then might be expected to measure quality of life.

Another criticism is that life-satisfaction responses reflect the dominant view on life, rather than actual quality of life in a country. So, life satisfaction is seen as a judgement that depends on social and culturally aspects, but this relativism is disproved by the fact that people in different countried report similar criteria as being important for life satisfaction, and by the fact that most differences in life satisfaction across countries can be explained by differences in objective circumstances. In addition, it has been found that the responses of immigrants in a country are much closer the level of the local population than to responses in their motherland.

In the view point of economists, who disagree to take the survey results completely at face value and use the average score on life satisfaction as the indicator of quality of life for a country. There are several reasons. First, comparable results for a sufficient number of countries tend to be out -of -date and many nations are not covered at all. Second, the impact of measurement errors on assessing the relationship indicators tends to cancel out across a large number of countries. But these might still be significant errors for any given country. So, there is a bigger chance of error in assessing quality of life between countries if we take a single average life satisfaction score as opposed to a multi-component index. Finally, and most important reason, although most of the inter-country variation in the life satisfaction surveys can be explained by objective factors, there is still a significant unexplained component which, in addition to measurement error, might to related to specific factors, that we want to net out from an objective quality of life index.

Instead environment protection product firms can attempt to use the survey results as a starting point, and a means for deriving weights for the various determinants of quality of life across countries, in order to calaulate an objective index. The average scores from comparable life-satisfaction surveys (on a scale of one to ten) can be assembled for 1999 year or 2000 year in a multi-variate regression to various factors satisfaction in many studies. Together these variables explain more than 80% of the inter-country variation in life-satisfaction scores. The surveys showed the weights of the various factors, included health, material well-being, and political stability and security. These were followed by family relations and community life. Next, in order of importance were climate (environment factor), job security, political freedom and finally gender equality. The surveys showed that the values of the life-satisfaction scores that are predicted by nine indicators represent a country's quality of life index or the corrected life-satisfaction scores, based on objective cross-country determinants. The method also means that the original units or measurement of the various indicators can be rely on the potentially distortive effect of having to transform all indicators to a common measurement also. The survey results indicate the determinents of quality of life factors, and the indicators used to represent these factors are: material wellbeing, health, political stability and security, family life, community life, climate and geography (environment factor), job security (unemployment rate), political freedom, gender equality. However, a number of other variables were also investigates but, upward trend in average life-satisfaction scores in developed nations, whereas average income has grown substantially. However, there is no evidence for an explanation that it has relationship between increasing incomes and stagnant life-satisaction scores: otherwise, the idea that an increase in someone's income causes enemy or disadvantage and reduces the welfare and satisfaction of others. In the researchers' estimates the level of income inequality had no impact on levels of life satisfaction , life satisfaction is primarily determined by absolute, rather than relative, status (related to states of mind and aspirations).

The explanation is that there are factors associated with modernisation that, in part offest its positive impact, such as crime, and drug and alcohol addiction, a decline in political participation and of trust in public authority, the erosion of the institutions of family and marriage. In personal terms, this has also been manifested in increased general uncertainty and personal risk. These pheonomena have accompanied rising incomes and expanded individual choice (both of which are highly valued). However stable family life and community are also highly valued and these have undergone a severe erosion. The survey results also showed that four of the indicators are forecast for 2005 yar (GDP , life expectancy, unemployment rate, political stabiliy); one geography is fixed and the remaining four, which represent slow changing factors and quality of life has relationship.

Thus, the researchers implied that GDP method is not accurate to measure human's quality of life. It ought have those other different methods to measure human's quality of life, such as survey method etc. as well as income is not only one factor to influence material wellbeing of human's quality of life; there are other different variable factor to influence human's quality of life, such as health, political stability, security, family of life, community life, climate and geography (environment factor), job security (unemployment rate), political freedom, gender equality etc. factors.

McGregor & Goldsmith (1998) explained that " quality is life is relative and difference between individuals, but it can be perceived as the level of satisfaction or confidence with one's conditions, relationships and surroundings relative to the available alternatives. The concept of quality of life is multifaceted. Quality of life consists of among other things: hope for the future, land, adequate food, clothing, shelter, income, employment opportunities, maternal and child health, and family and social welfare." The concept of quality of life is indeed multi-dimersional, complex and very subjective. For example, someone who has changed their consumptin habit to better ensure that their choices with make a better quality of life for themselves, the environment and future generations, may be seen by others as having a lower or inferior quality of life since which have removed themselves from the materialistic mainstream characteristics of our consumer society. Someone may feel that an absence of violence and abuse in their life and natural fresh air and clean water good quality supply can lead to even though who have fewer tangible resources, money or shelter; peace of mind and freedom from abuse has increased the quality of their daily life relative to what it was like before.

Otherwise, standard of living is often equated with quality of life, but it is not the same thing. A standard of life is a way of life to which a group of people are accustomed. Some people's standard of living includes only basic food, clothing, shelter and safety. Other people expect to eat at expensive restaurants, wear designer clothes, live in huge homes and travel extensively. Different people expect and want different things, who have different standards, which are very much shaped by values, goals, money, past experience and socialization. However, standard of living are most commonly assessed in terms of annual household income levels and to a lesser extent, wealth, community assistance, family contributions, special family needs, distribution of income within the family or household and geographic location.

Thus, it seems that standard of living or GDP alone is not a good measure of quality of life. Quality of life is a personal and inward looking concept that has both objective (factual) and subjective (perception) components.

However, an individual's quality of life is also affected by external factors (build and natural environment; services and facilities) and this directly links quality of life to regional issues. The subjective aspect of quality of life is particularly important as if reflects how people feel about their situation and this can't be gauged from objective indicators. Subjective quality of life is often broken down into seven life domains: standard of living, health, achievements in life, personal relationships, safety, community connection and future security. For example, the measure of domain, such as standard of living includes as on income and wealth and housing aspect. The subjective measures: satisfaction with standard of living, distribution with wealth in the region, perceptions of personal income, wealth, housing affordability, housing density, green space and facilities near to homes. Objective measures may include distribution of income, welfare dependence, levels of housing stress. On health aspects, the subjective measures , satisfaction with personal health, region's health services, self assessed health status, needs and service usage. Objective measures may include services available per capita, suicide rates . It seems environment pollution factor can be one part to influence human quality of life.

Many studies of quality of life suggest that personal relations are an importnt aspect, or perhaps the most important aspect of quality of life. For example, Cornelia, B.F. (1999) found that change in interpersonal relations appear to contribute more heavily to satisfaction with quality of life than does either socioeconomic status or social participation. Who found that quality of life is not related of living, having choices is the productive work that you do is the most important dimension of quality of life. However, on environment aspect, rural development is most effective in increasing quality of life when it can increase diversity, both in the environment and in the economy,which can increase social capital, the norms and networks that provide for a collective identity and mutual respect. It can also increase standard of living. Efforts need to promoted standard of quality of life may have.

In fact, every American community with the problem of balancing environment growth with the need to maintain environmental and social health. For example, efficient agriculture to businesses get information about new technologies to present pollution. Increasing role of quality of life and standard of living took place in countries all over the world, especially nowadays, when numerous affects of the global crisis are felt all over the world. Emerging crisis caused many problems. thereby, in the current situation, it is interesting to examine the level of the quality of life and standard of living. After short overview of general development of concepts of standard of living and quality of life. The different indicators can measure quality of life or standard of living include GDP per capita, shopping basket, GFK basket, households' expenditures, poverty rate, income inequality, life satisfaction and happiness etc. indicators. The measures show an increase in the standard of living and quality of life. Hence, if the result showed the standard of living and quality of life. The high level of human development and the results of the level of satisfaction imply that human are moderately satisfied with their lives and enjoy a rather high level of happiness.

Standard of living and quality of life have been concerning issues in countries for many years, especially nowadays, when numersous effects of the global crisis are felt all over the world. The financial security and prosperity of the economic systems disappeared. The economic storm caused rising unemployment, falling incomes, increasing rates of poverty and declines in overall well-being. Thereby, in the current situation, it is interesting to examine quality of life and standard of living. However, standard of living is defined and the level of welfare available to individual or to the group of people. It concerns products and services, people are able to consume and the recources who have access too. It depends on the quality and quantity of available products and services and the way who are distributed within the population. Otherwise, standard of living is generally determined by indicators, such as real income per person and poverty rate. Quality of life indicates to the overall welfare within a certain society, focused on enabling each member on opportunity of accomplishing objectives. Unlike the concept of standard of living, quality of life refers to not only indicators of material standard, but also to various subjective factor that influence human lives, such as natural environment pollution challenges. However, in the estimation of standard of living and quality of life their are used two types of measures, objective and subjective indicators. Objective indicators are used to determine and to explain the economic segment, when subjective indicators are used as a descriptive indicator of the noneconomic segment of quality of life and standard of living.

Many researchers were done in the field of economics, psychology, clinicial medicine, health care, phiolsophy and social science to measure whether which kind of factors can cause human quality of life to be poor. The understanding of the concepts passed through a long period of evolution. Human need natural resources have enough supply to able to satisfy their needs. It concerns the physical circumstances, such as natural environment in which people live, the products and service who are able to consume and the resources who have access to. So, the good quality of life which depends on the quantity and quality of available products and services and their distribution within the population. Otherwise, the idea of standard of living requires a macro perspective and it is generally measured by standards, such as real income per person and poverty rate. The most common measure is national output per capita, measured such as GDP or GDP per capita. Other measures, such as income inequality and life satisfaction are also used. So, it can be feeling of human intangible measure, psychological feeling to measure quality of life to human. It seems that the environmental pollution can have close relationship to influence human quality of life. Thus, quality of life can be measured by objective as well as subjective indicators. One researcher, Felce and Perry (1995) who defined quality of life is as total welfare which includes objective and subjective evaluation of physical, material, social and emotional welfare, personal development and activity, all together evaluated throughout personal set of values

What are objective indicators of standard of living and quality of life? Objective circumstances refer to the economic and material conditions which are important aspects of the standard of living and quality of life. In the assessment, eight different indicators were used: CPI, GDP per capita, shopping basket, household's expenditures, GFIC basket, poverty rate, income inequality and HDI. However, these indicators is one number measure. It can't measure anyone's psychological feeling, such as health, safe emotion. The challenge concerns whether environmental pollution factor, such as air pollution, water pollution can cause human's health to be poor, even goes down human's quality of life and economy loss. I shall indicate some evidences to give reasons to support my conclusion why I believe that environment pollution is a factor to cause human quality of life to be poor , even it can also cause economy will encounter loss too.

In general, measure of quality of life need include human's psychological feeling indicator. I shall indicate, Hong Kong, China countries air and water environmental pollution challenges how to influence these two countries' people quality of life to be poor, even, it will cause their economy loss. Nowadays, China and Hong Kong and India and Afria are encountering health problems arising from damage to lungs, heart and blood vessels. Hong Kong and India and Afria and China e.g. Shanghai city pollution is a significant cause of premature death from cardiopulmonary disorders. Present level of pollution cause injury to the immature developing lings of children and adolescents. This damage will lead to life-long health problems in many and a reduction in life-expectancy. Although, there is no evidence from analyses of trends in pollutants that pollution measures in recent years have reduced pollutant concentrations in a way which will benefits public health.

There are clear indicators that for some pollutants. The problem is worsening. In fact, air and water pollution is Hong Kong and China and Afria etc. developing countries' the biggest cause of social and environmental injustice. It harms not only citizens today, but because its transquenerational effects on the urborn and youngest members of the society, it will cause its will health effects well into the later years of this century, even environmental pollution challenge will cause these countries will encounter economy loss. Thus, these above countries can give more chance to any environment protection products to sell their products to any cities, which are encountering environment pollution challenges.

Human activities have created forms of air and water pollution, such as gases from fuels, uncontrolled emissons from fossil fuels and other chemical sources have long been recognized as a cause of ill health and premature death. For example, in December, 1930 year, a dense fog affected the Meuse Valley in Belgium. Beginning on December, 3 date, the fog intensified over three days and was associated with laryngeal symptoms, chest pain, coughing, and breathlessness. Some patients showed signs of pulmonary oedema. Overall 60 deaths were attributed to the episode. After a long investigation, the cause was considered to be emissions from high sulphur fuels, including suplhur dioxide and sulphuric acid.

What is the current threat to health? the migigration of air polluton following the introduction of clear air has been followed by a period of unprecedented economic development creating new forms of pollution from the combustion of fossil fuels. For example, in constrast to the relatively large tar laden particulates from burning dirty coal which caused episodes like the London city, UK. Smog , traffic pollution now genertes fine with a different size and composition and gases,such as which may cause injury to the respiratory system and the effects of other pollutants. Such as particulates and drive the formation of the secondary pollutant ozone. The effects of pollution will therefore to some extent reflect genetic, environmental lifestyle and behavioral factors to develop these distance in a population together with the existing prevalence of diseases which may be polluted. Hence, living in polluted urban environments is associated with increased levels of biological markers of inflammation compared with residence in a clean air environment. The damage is caused by air pollution manifests itself through a variety of common and recognized health problems, such as upper complaints heart and lung disease. Because of this, we can use statistical methods as well as clinical studies to detect the signal of changes in health problems and increased health care demands in the population. However, doctors had proved air or water pollution can cause these both curdiovscular or respiratory disease indirectly. Curdiovscular disease includes formation of arterial plaques, coronary artery, heart attacks, irregular heart rhythm, loss of heart rate variability, high blood pressure, stroke etc. disease. Respiratory disease includes inflammation of nasal, throat and tracheal airways with acute, lower respiratory tract inflammation and infection causing bronchitis, reduction long growth and function in young people. So, it seems environmental pollution can influence quality of life to human as well as environmental pollution and illness and poor health problem has close relationship.

On the other side, envionmental pollution can bring health risk, over it will influence social inequalities. Some researchers had found that the evidence has been compiled for six envionmental health challenges, such as air quality, housing and residential location, unintentional injuries in children, work related health risks, waste management and climate change. It seems human need to concern air and drinking water quality, waste management and climate change how to influence our environmental pollution challenge. Although, the evidence base on social inequalities and environmental risk is fragmented and data are often available for few countries only, it indicates that inequalities are a major challenge for environmental health policies. Irrespective of development status, environmental inequalities can be found in any country for which data are available. The valid for the exposure to environmental risk factor is also unequally distributed, and this unequal distribution is often related to social characteristics, such as income, social status, employment and education, even environment risk factor can influence human's quality of life.

How environmental risk factor can influence different groups
However, environment protection product firms need to concern how environmental risk factor can influence inequally health outcomes to different groups. Such as, the first group is social determinants affect the environmental conditions of an individual and may contribute to the fact that specific individuals or population groups more often experience loss adequate or potentially harmful environmental conditions. The second group is the affected population groups could still be more exposed through e.g. the mechanism of education and health behavior. The third group is given socially disadvantaged groups could show more severe health effects of the social disadvantage is associated. The final group is social determinants affect health (what remains unclear is the relative importance of socially determined exposure to environmental risk factors). Thus, any manufacturers need to concern how whose behavior can lead environmental pollution to influence poor health to alive, due to whose productive process. Even, every country's citizen themselves can not neglect how to protect our natural environment to be clean issue. Due to environmental unhealth poor issue can lead our bodies to be unhealth and to be ill and we have no health to work to influence our job inefficiency and low productivity if we often need to see doctor to raise workload to my staffs often. Then, employers will be probable to consider to attempt to buy any environmental protection products to reduce or avoid pollution occurrence to influence loss of legal compensation from the different social groups' complain. Hence, employers will cosiderate environmental justice and environmental inequity issue, e.g. how to reduce indoor air

pollution and occupational or exposure to environmental tobacco smoke pollution exposure to high traffic roads or to industrial plants pollution to influence different social groups' health challenges. So, the environmental protection product firms' clients , who can include social different target groups and any product manufacturers.

How Afria country environmental pollution influences

Surprisingly, most of above countries , among of them, although Africa is a green and natural environmental country, but Africa has encounted poor natural environmental quality to influence it has poor quality of life to its citizen and poor economy growth to its society both. Why does Africa encounter this natural environmental pollution challenge? Afican have now two potential sources of pollution: consumption and production . This looks reasonable to Africa, since maintenance is completely dedicated to improving the environment, when production generates pollution only as a " by product". Capital implies the possibility of a country being trappical in an economent poverty trap by both a bad environment and low longevity. Some countries (or regions) may even experience other time, both environmental degradation and decay in expectancy. The fact that, in some cases, environmental degradation doesn't imply lower longevity may be due to the fact that economic growth might , at the same time, worsen environmental quality, but generate additional resources that can help increasing (or preserving) longevity. However, these is also evidence of countries where environmental degradation is associated with a reduction in life expectancy. It seems worsen environmental quality will influence any country's economic growth and poor quality of life both. For example, McMichael et al. (2004) identify 40 countries that experienced a loss in longevity between 1990 year and 2001 year (26 between 1980 year and 2001), they also support that the resulting world divergence in terms of life expectancy might be explained by "…. (the growing) health risks consequent on large-scale environmental changes is caused by human pressur, by both bad environment and low longevity, biodiversity and sustainable energy".

How human adult consumption and environmental quality influences future environment for human survival probability of life expectancy.

I shall assure human adult consumption and environmental quality has relationship to influence the future environment (green preferences) to provide human survival probability, it depends on inherited environmental quality. Thus, human will increase or decrease in the survival probability when we need a higher or lower life expectancy. In general, we depend on these environmental conditions to live, which include quality of water, air and soils etc. and resource availability, biodiversity, forestry, fisheries etc.

It is interesting to analyze different possible strategies to escape from the environmental poverty trap as well as factors that could push some economies back to a low equilibrium characterized. To research whether environment factor has relationship to influence human quality of life. We need to give idea of explaining whether environmental care has relationship to an uncertain lifetime. However, I suppose that an environmental kind of factor can be instead of being defined in terms of GDP per capita, capital accumulation etc. economic factors. Poverty is now related to environmental quality. It should be clear, however, I focus only on one specific mechanism lying behind environmental traps. Just as under development traps may be related to a wide variety of factors, ranging from financial to technological ones, including human capital accumulation and life expectancy. So, I should use this assumption to explain why it has relatively between environmental quality and life expectancy.

This " synthetic" indicator (YCELP, 2006) indicated environmental health is defined by child morality, indoor air polluton, drinking water, adequate sanitation and urban particulates and ecosystem vitality that includes factors like air quality, water and productive natural resources, A key ingredient of our setting is that survival until the last period is probabilistic and depends on the inherited quality of the environments. This survival probability affects the weight of the future environmental quality in human's utility function to achieve interest aim. Final stage, human will have optimal choices depend on life expectancy: in particular, a higher probability to be alive in the third period boosts investment in the environment and reduces consumption. In this case, a given country may be caught in a high morality/poo environment if low income is associated with a deteriorated environment.

John and Pecchenino (1994) were the first to introduce the possibility of multiple identifying, case for a poverty cause characteristic by poor economic performance and environmental degradation, however, life expectancy is assumed to be exogenous and plays no role in their model. Such as soils deterioration are the like, are all susceptible of increasing human morality (thus reducing longevity). So, the existence of both environmental performance and longevity, with countries being concentrated around two levels of environmental quality and life expectancy respectively. The two-way causes are between the environment and longevity. If the causal relationship between environmental quality and life expectancy involves the existence of an environmental poverty, characterized by both bad environmental conditions and short life expectancy.

Human life stage will encounter generations of three periods to get utility from consumption and environmental quality. During adulthood, when all relevant decisions are taken, adult can work and allocate their income between consumption and investment in environmental maintenance: consumption involves deterioration of the future quality of the environment (through pollution and/or resource depletion) when maintenance helps to improve it. The dynamics of environmental quality may also be affected by external factors on more resourced communities. The most importance, unhealthy physical environments across the region adversely affect everyone, ever though who are likely to be most concentrated in more burdened community which also have less social power to change those environments.

Why life expectancy and the environment has close relationship to influence quality of life? Life expectancy and environmental quality dynamics are jointly determined. Human may invest in environmental quality, depending on how much , we expect to live. However, environmental conditions affects life expectancy. In particular, some countries may encounter in a low life expectancy / low environmental quality. This outcome is consistent with stylized facts relating life expectancy and environmental performance measures. Some expects to live longer, who would be willing to invest more in environmental quality, because who feel which have causal link between life expectancy and environmental quality. However, environmental quality is a very important factor affecting health and morbidity: air and water pollution, depletion of natural resources and quality of life.

Why social and physical environmental factors have close relationship to influence economic growth

I shall indicate reasons to explain why social and physical environmental factors have close relationship to influence economic growth, even human health of quality of life. The social and economic burdens of poor education, lack of affordable housing and less than self sufficient income affect, not just those individuals and families who have the fewest resources. The social gradient means that not only do whose in the bottom worse health outcomes to bottom of income group and the top income group whose will have poor quality of life influence. The higher rates of disease and disability and lesser productivity among many communities means a higher public and private burden of life years, particularly life expectancy once one reaches age 65. In recent decades, research and has increasingly shown how powerfully social and economic conditions determine population health and differences in health among subgroups, much more so than medical care. It seems that environmental factor can influence human's quality of life.

Los Angeles Country Department Of public Health (2016) indicated a country health rankings model, this department explained these three health factors can cause this health outcomes. These health factors include health behaviors (30%), it includes tobacco use, diet and exercise, alcohol use, unsafe sex; clinical care (20%), it includes access to care, quality of care; social and economic factors (40%), it includes education, employment, income, family and social support, community safety; physical environmental factor (10%) , includes natural environmental quality, built environmental quality. Then these factors can cause this health outcomes, such as morality (length of life):50% and morbidity (quality of life) :50%. SO, it implies that physical environmental factor can influence human's length of life. So, on our social environmental problems result is from a complex interplay of a number of forces. An individual's health −related behaviors , particularly diet, exercise and smoking, surrounding physical environment and health care (both access and quality) all contribute significantly to how long and how well human love. However , none of these factors is as important to population health as are the social and economic environments in which human live, learn, work and play. We refer to these factors can be as the social determinants of health to influence our quality of life. How do social determinants affect our quality of life? In the late 19th and early 20th centuries, public health concentrated particularly on the physical environment. Improvements in, for example, clean water supplies, healthier housing, sanitation, workplace safety and safe food lead to sharp increases in average life expectancy . Also our quality of life needed to be concentrated on expanded access to medical care, resulting in further expansion. So, the poverty tap is now characterized by those elements, such as low levels of : (i) environmental quality, (ii) life expectancy and (iii) human capital.

In fact, environmental degradation can have a significant impact on human health. De Hollander et. al (1999) & Melse & De Hollander (2001) showed that estimates of the share of environment, related human health loss are as high 5% for high income countries, 8% for middle income countries and 13% for low income countries. Air pollution and exposure to hazardous chemicals are important causes of the related burden of disease in countries. The transport and energy sectors are major contributors to air pollution, when important sources of chemical pollution are agriculture industry and waste disposal. Opportunities for reducing environment-related health risks are considerable. The benefits of many environment policies in terms of reduced health care costs and increased productivity significant exceed the costs of implementing those policies. So, the impact of environmental risk factors on health are extremely varied and complex. For example, the effects of environmental degradation on human health can range from death caused by cancer, due to air pollution to psychological problems resulting from noise. So it implies environmental factor can influence our quality of life in our societies. However, many factors can also influence human's health of a population, including diet, sanitation, socio-economic status, literacy and lifestyle.

De Hollander et. al. (1999) & Melse and De Hollander (2001) showed that total burden of disease, with estimated environment-related share expenditure, mid-1990 year. The average income group has 15 daily/1000 capita, the middle income group has 20 daily/1000 capita, the high income group has 10 daily/1000 capita. As regards both total burden of disease and the health conditions related to environmental; degradation. The result indicates the environment –related share of the burden of disease is greatly dependent on income, with higher-environmental shares generally occurring in lower-income countries.

On the one hand, it seems the large environmental share of health problems is primarily, due to factors related to poverty, such as limited to access to proper food, housing, health care and drinking water. Environmental determinants of human health in developing or developed countries are related. On the other hand, those to the exposure to air pollutants (particularly in urban areas and chemicals in the environment than to poor living conditions. Also sources of human exposure to chemicals are many and varied. Chemicals can reach the environments, for example, through emissions from industries, anti-fouling paints on marine vessels, pesticides in agriculture, waste incineration and leakage from waste disposal sites. When emissions of chemicals from industries and other point sources of pollution have lead to poor quality of life, source of chemical exposure. Intensive agricultural production uses chemicals in pesticides and fertilizer and in feed additives and medication for livestock. Residues remain in fruit, grains, vegetables, meats and daily products, all of which can reach the consumer.

Other sources of chemicals in food include bio-accumulative chemicals in the environment, such as heavy metals and persistent organic pollutants, which can be found in fish, meat and dairy products. So, environment pollution can influence human need to eat bad or unhealthy food to cause we have poor quality of life to live, such as the high income group or middle income group or low income group of families in our societies fairly. Other human health risks that have recently received considerable attention include unsafe livestock feeding practices through which toxins reach the food chain unintentionally. Dioxins that have accidentally contaminated poultry feeds that contain diseased animal remains can cause the so-called " mad cow disease" in livestock which has been linked to a new form of disease. The effects on health from exposure to chemicals and air pollutants vary from allergies to cancer. Although, the link between exposure and disease is often not clear, Even at low exposure levels, urban are pollutants can cause, asthma, allergies, respiratory diseases and cardiovascular disease if the exposure is continuous or long term. Heavy metals have been shown to cause neurological disorders and various cancers. In addition to , physical diseases, environmental contamination can also cause psychological problems. Noise, one of the determinants of the quality of urban life can have an impact on human health, decreasing the quality of life and potentially contributing to depression.

For Ireland, UK country example, this country politicians and policy makers believe the role of environment can be used to measure quality of life, concerning on either in its own right or relative to economic and social aspects of quality of life. Agreement on what measures quality of life and how it can be measured by the role of environment, not just in Ireland, but everywhere. The conventional approach is used for policy has been to use measure of gross domestic product(GDP) or regional valued added. However, it is acknowledged that such conventional economic measures have only a partial relationship with societal wellbeing. To the extent that economic measures are related to public products and consumption, there are also pressing issues in relation to public products and the sustainability of economic growth. However, the role of environmental factor can influence resource use and human's behavioral consumption.

Aspects to quality of life other than income include the environment, freedom, health, working condition, leisure, social and family relationship. Economists don't deny that these factors do play a role in quality of life. However, environment factor can be one role to influence other factors to influence our quality of life to be good or bad effect. For example, locations which might be desirable as paces to life (in terms of income earning opportunities or other factors) were also likely to have higher costs of living, particularly with regard to house prices or health or unhealthy air/water pollution of environment situation of the place to provide human to live. Alternatively, social indicators are based on normative ideals of literacy, low rates of premature mortality or a quality environment. Other measurement of people's personal evaluation of their quality of life, much depends on personal expectations and experience.

How environmental factor can influence any country's house price.

I shall indicate that why environmental factor will influence any country's house price. For Ireland example, citizen average incomes and higher in the east of the country, house prices are lower in the west, who are also more able to afford a property of choices. There are more opportunities to purchase houses, where people own their own houses, who are more likely to have benefits from an appreciation is its value and to consequently perceive a higher degree of health. Generally, levels of property appreciation have been higher in the east. Unfortunately, young people and the more economically active segment of the population are more likely to be faced with rising entry level house prices and the prospect of large borrowings. So, the quality of life, such as education, crime and access to healthcare and living environment are not uniformly better in the west or the east regions. Indeed, many measures of social disadvantage are at their worst in the west regions. Some indicators of environmental quality are , indeed better in the west regions, but there are others, such as drinking-water quality or recreational access that are often worse.

Comparisons can often be reduced to an urban-rural dimension rather than a regional one. Factors such as incomes, house prices, crime levels, air pollution and congestion are all likely to be higher in urban areas in Ireland city, UK country. Why environment and housing price has relationship in Ireland to influence quality of life to its citizen? If Ireland's regional development policy is successful , it will bring with it greater competition in the housing market and greater pressures on the environment in Ireland. Because the forest will be decreased to build house, the natural environment will become wood and steel and stone of housing built environment. In fact, it appears that there is a fair of amount of agreement on the relative rating of factors influencing quality of life. Ability to own one's home and security of income were needed, but respondents also placed almost equal important on clean air and drinking water, low crime were differences. The Ireland's rural respondents appeared to place a slightly greater emphasis on key natural environmental attributes, when urban residents valued absolute incomes and social or leisure activity rather more.

In this respect, the analysis identifies three components to Ireland people of quality of life, each of which was evident in all three locations. There components can be broadly described as domestic security, social/leisure and aspects of the planned environment. The first of these includes indicators, such as security of income, absolute income, house ownership and low crime. As this component includes air and drinking-water quality, it suggests that these indicators may be associated with personal health and well-being. When the planned environment component includes those attributes that affect quality of life over which the authorities have a direct influence, for instance, a clean environment, traffic and reducing vehicle numbers on the roads in busy time. Hence, environmental protection product firms can find anywhere the houses price are going down, it is possible that the pollution factor influences who choose to live there. So it implies that the locations of house buyers will have more needs to buy their environmental protection products protect whose health if who need to live these locations.

How environmental pollution can influence social welfare

Environmental quality has an undefined impact on quality of life and various indicators are used to show regional variations in aspects, such as water quality . There are many measures of environmental quality , but is only for quality of life. Moreover, the measurement of societal welfare is important. Societal welfare is not simply , the sum of the parts, but varies depending on the individual in which people find themselves at any time in their life. In principle, it should be possible to apply weights to each element of societal welfare, but as preferences for each of these vary within the population. In the absence of a method with which everybody is satisfied, GNP and GDP are typically the most popular used measures for quality of life or standard of life. But, these are problems with the data itself to measure quality of life because quality of life is feeling or satisfaction of level to the country's citizen and it can not be seen by numbers or statistic method. For example, GDP ignores household production, such as the effort that goes into the rearing of children, the benefits that this provides for society and the public expenditure that is avoided. Neither are costs treated equally with the benefits. GDP counts all economical activities irrespective on pollution appears to increase. GDP even through it is a degree of double counting.

Otherwise, environmental products are good to be measured to quality of life. For example, many environmental products are unpriced. Consequently, environmental products that people value, or which are critical to the sustainability of development, are abused or depleted because of their public products have good characteristics and the absence of a market price signal.

Environmental economists try to work within the economic model to measure quality of life. Rather than questioning the link between utility and consumption or choice, the preferred approach is to add an element into the utility function that represents the value of environmental products or the stock of natural capital. By one means or another , the preservation value of these environmental products is estimated in terms of willingness to pay to protect the environment or as willingness to forego other products in return. It seems the quality of people's environment can be represented by objective indicators. At another, their interpretation will vary and can be represented by subjective indicators. So, enviromental products can have economic benefits to provide social welfare to citizen to live in any countries.

Objective indicators come in two forms: (i) economic indicators and (ii) social indicators. The former depends on an ability to select the environmental products and services that are desires, in other words, the satisfaction of preferences . The economic argument is that people select the best quality of life, who can obtain commensurate with their resources and personal desires. By comparison, social indicators are based on normative ideals on what could be considered the food life. For example, would be infant morality, literacy, crime rates and social indicators are objective measures. Both have guided, much of the research on quality of life, particularly concerning with the urban environment. Quality of life can include natural a significant influence on local quality of life, for instance, natural beauty spots used for recreation.

For environmental quality concept, it concerns with health, safety, wellbeing, residential satisfaction and the physical sustainability can be considered to result from an when live ability can be considered to represent the interaction between the physical and the social domains. As with expenditure on the environment, investment in social capital contributes to quality of life. However, the benefits will again vary amongst individuals, depending largely on the security of their individual circumstance. As with the environment, the government can certainly adopt strategies that provide for public security by taking measures to reduce crime, a measure likely to be appreciated by everybody (except criminal) , at least to one degree or another. In other necessary to enhance social interaction, namely community centers or sports facilities. Furthermore, the creation of social capital has an statement which responds to general social trends to raise Ireland citizen's quality of life.

I shall indicate Ireland to explain whether environmental factor is the main factor to influence our quality of life and economic growth. Is environmental quality higher in the Ireland west regions? And if so, does this compensate for lower incomes in these regions? Is it bad that rural areas are characterized by higher costs of living in areas other than housing by environmental factor? In fact, in Ireland , UK country, population increase has a direct impact on the environment by placing demands on local natural resources, particularly open space and water. It also leads to a sense of crowding that reduces the utility associated with access to the environment. How can environment factor influence economy growth in Ireland? In Ireland, agriculture has gone through a period of significant change that has been accelerated reductions in the amount of mixed cropping and traditional land management. Indeed, changes in the expectations of young farmers will ensure that further change is likely to be characterized by increases in farm size and greater specialization with implications for landscape and wildlife. These characteristics of farm holdings are more familiar in the east regions of Ireland , UK country. As with likely to extend to the west regions as the older generation of farmers retires, although this will probably be accompanied by a trend to more farming of production needs to young farmers. So, good natural environment can provide Ireland young farmers to produce more agriculture to earn income, even who can export more rice, fruits, vegetable etc. agriculture foods to overseas. Hence, Ireland GDP will be raise if it can have good natural resource environment to provide Ireland young farmers to grow foods to sell to domestic and /or foreign agricultural market. Given the rate of economic growth, and its concentration in the east of the Ireland, UK country, it would be easy to presume that the quality of the environment is higher the further away from the mid east one goes. Thus, good natural environment is an important factor to influence the farming industry development in Ireland , UK county to satisfy their needs and to raise their quality of life nowadays. It implies that environmental protective products have more needs to any farming to use in Ireland, UK country.

I shall indicate New Zealand and America two developed countries to explain why which are facing environmental pollution challenge to influence their citizen's quality of life and economic growth nowadays. The first country is NZ, although, New Zealand is a developed and natural environmental country, but it had been envountering air pollution annouance and noise annoyance to influence it's citizen's health-related quality of life. I shall indicate why which has this relationship between of them in New Zealand. Nowadays, New zealand population growth is an increasing demand for consumer products and urbanization have lead to concerns over the lived environments in many of the world's cities, such as Auckland, wellington cities in New Zealand. However, environmental quality is an important determinant of health, such as the bad influence of traffic-related air and noise pollution on health outcomes, specially with respect to at risk groups, both in relation to long term exposure as well as acute effect, from brief exposures. For example, cholesterol levels and in relation to myocardial infaction. Nowadays, New Zealand is encountering the high degree of air pollution and noise annoyance to influence it's citizen's quality of life. Air pollutants can be detected either visually, such as witnessing smoke emanating from a vehicles's exhaust, or by smell, such as when odorants stimulate olfactory receptors. The evidence linking air pollution to adverse impacts on human health.

Many air impacts on human health. Many air pollution health studies have focused specifically on urban area, and vehicle generated pollution in particular, as road vehicles are one of the major sources of pollution across much of the world. Elemental carbon, Nox and ultrafine particles an considered to be pollutants most strongly associated with road traffic emissions. In Auckland and Wellington cities, New Zealand , it has been estimated that 71% of summer and 21% of winter concentrations of fine particulate matter is attributable to motor vehicles. Moreover, poor town planning decisions in Auckland (and in New Zealand in general) over many decedes has meant that may people live in very close proximity to busy road and motorways within " road corridors" and so are the adverse effects of road traffic, including noise and air pollution as well as experiencing on potential for degradation in their quality of life. Such as, New Zealand is highly suitable for studies investigating the impact of roads on the health of its residents. For example, NZ, road traffic noise and aviation noist has been linked to cardiovascular disease, hypertension and ischemic heart disease. It influences NZ resident personal psychological and physical both health challenges. In fact, NZ noise increases morbidity and mortality independently of air pollution exposure, though air pollution constituted a greater burden of disease when arise exposure had a greater impac on quality of life, e.g. NZ road traffic noise and air pollution will be caused from drivers in busy time. Specially in Auckland and Wellington cities. It will influence urban and rural environmental pollution. Some retired old people who will feel annoyance when this road traffic occurs in Auckland or Wellington cities to close to their houses in transportation busy time every day.

Next developed country is America, this country's air pollution is also serious nowadays. Because traffic jam often occurs in New York, Washington, Boston etc. big cities in US. So, U.S. cities' parks and its trees have significant influence to produce fresh air to provide U.S. residents who are living in cities to breach for their body health. David J. & Gordon , M. (2016) indicated " In U.S. these urban parks are estimated to contain about 370 million trees with a structural value of approximately $300 billion." The number of park trees varies by region of the country, but which can produce significant air quality effects in and near parks, related to air temperatures, air pollution, ultraviolet indication and carbon dioxide (a dominant greenhouse gas related to global climate change). Additional open space and other vacant lands in cities, which may contain trees and other vegatation. Contribute significant additional benefits, effects of parks and open space at the city scale can vary significantly depending on the amount of parkland and amount of tree cover within the parkland.

The reasons why parks can reduce air pollution. Parks generally have lower air temperature than surrounding areas. Temperatures are usually cooler toward the center of a park than around its edges. At night, the center of a large park may be 13 degree cooler than surrounding city areas. The cooler air from parks often moves out into adjacent developed neighborhoods. This cooling of surrounding areas tends to increase with park size and percentage of the park covered by trees. So, cooler air temperature is provided by urban parks can have significant impacts on human health. During heat wave events, which can kill hundreds of people, park areas may provide city dwellers with some respite from high air temperture, particularly in the evening, during hot, sunny days tree shade can greatly increase human comfort. Because park influences on air temperature extend to developed areas outside of parks, local energy use for heating and cooling buildings is also effected. Although, the net around effect of parks on energy costs has been by reducing temperature is difficult to estimate at least in the southern United States the effect will usually be a net annual benefit. Futhermore, large park trees will reduce winds and may provide a benefit of winter heating of buildings near the park. Although, the overall economic effect of urban trees and parks on air temperature reduction is not fully billions of dollars annually at the national scale in terms of improved environmental quality and human health.

In fact, trees and vegetation in parks can help reduce air pollution both by directly removing pollutants and by reducing air temperatures and building energy use in and near parks. There tree effects can reduce pollutant emissions and formation. However, park vegetation can increase some pollutants by either directly emitting volatile orgnic compounds that can contribute to ocone and carbon monoxide formation or indirectly by the emission of air pollutants through vegetation maintenance practices, such as operation of chain and use of transportation fuels. David J. & Gordon , M. (2016) showed "Annual pollution removal and economic benefits by U.S. urbank park trees is estimated at about 75,000 tones ($500 million) or 80 pounds per acre of tree cover ($300 per acre of tree cover). Carton storage and annual removal by urban park trees and soils in the United States is estimated at about: carton storage trees: 75 million tons ($1.6 billion), carton storage (soils) : $102 million tons of carbon removal (trees): 2.4 million tons ($50 million)". Park management is recommended by U.S. environment protection department: considering that most of the effects of trees on microclimate and air quality are beneficial for park users and nearby residents; park designs that include a variety of land cover, areas of dense trees, scattered trees and lawn are likely to provide the greatest opportunities for optimum physical comfort of visitors; increase the number of healthy trees (increase pollution removal and carbon storage); sustain existing tree cover (maintains pollution removal levels) and (carbon storage); maximize use of low volatile organic compound emitting trees reduces ozove and carbon monoxide formation; sustain large, healthy trees (large trees have greatest per tree effcts on pollution and carbon removal); using long-lived trees (reduces long term pollutant emissions from removal; reducing fossil fuel in maintaining vegetation reduces pollutant ans carbon emissions)." So, if US had many green parks, then which can reduce air pollution, also it can assist many travellers who prefer to travel to US to raise GDP travelling income growth generally. It imples, USA park players and NZ road users will have more needs to attempt to buy any environmental protective products.

(vii) What is consumer neuroscientific research method to predict consumer behavior?

The key motivation has not been possible to directly observe the mental processes when subjects perceive marketing stimuli, such as advertisement or when who make purchasing decisions. Despite the long history of consumer research, little is known about the neural representation of how marketing stimuli affects consumers' perceptions, their decision-making processes and their consumption experience.

In the past, consumer researchers had to rely on varying the stimuli , e.g. prices or packaging and context factors, e.g. putting subjects in a good or bad mood in order to measure participants' reactions , e.g. choice behavior or brand preference. However, same researchers suggest scientific tools can observe brain activity to predict consumers behavior (Ambler et al., 2000 and Shiv and Fedorikhin, 1999 et al).

However, some consumer psychologists showed advertising research studies have often pointed out the important role of emotions for advertisement memorization (Ambler, 2000). In advertising research, who suggest that emotion and ratio are represented in different hemispheres of the brain. Research on the neural representation of stimuli-induced emotions, however, could show that emotions are not only processed in the left brain hemisphere, but are also processed bilaterally (e.g. in the left and right hemispheres of such cortical structure.

Customer loyalty is as an example, which can be defined as " a deeply held commitment to rebuy or a preferred product/service consistently in the future (Oliver, 1999). Consumer loyalty is a popular predictable consumer behavior topic for marketing researches, early research tried to establish whether customer loyalty has impact on aspects of business performance (such as profit margin and sales).

Loyalty is a psychological construct that develops over-time during a learning process of the consumer. Thus, loyalty research can benefit from insights in neuroscience and neuro-economics about how learning processes are represented in the brain. Some brain psychologists also explained how people learn to be loyal. They showed the following three processes in order to learn to be loyal.

(1) The brain should be able to memorize and retrieve positive and negative outcomes of former decisions, such as positive experiences after choosing brand A over brand B.

(2) The brain should be able to predict several outcomes of choosing between alternatives (buying A or B).

(3) The brain needs to integrate the information from processes 1 and 2 into the decision process.

Thus, it seems any environment protective product firm needs to concern how to develop loyalty and advertment promotion method and commitment to let environment protection product consumers to have more confidence to choose to buy whose products or learn how to use whose environment protection services more easily.

Whether design factor can predict consumer behavior for environment protection product

Why environmental pollution and human right abuses has close relationship to influence quality of life and economic growth?

In fact, environment pollution and human right abuses has close relationship. It is clear that poverty situations and human rights abuses are worsened by environmental degradation. The result can influence poor human quality of life to the developing countries' people unfairly. There are these several abvious reasons: firstly, the exhaustion of natural resources leads to unemployment and emigration to cities; secondly, this affects the enjoyment and exercise of basic human rights. Environmental conditions contribute to a large extents to the spread of infections diseases. From the

4,400 million of people who live in developing countries, almost 60% lack basis health care services, a almost a third of these people have no access to safe water supply; thirdly, degradation poses new problems, such as environmental refugees. Environmental refugees suffer from significant economic, socio-cultural and political consequences. And fourthly, environmental degradation worsens existing problems suffered by developing and developed countries. David J. Nowak & Gordon M. Melsler (2016) showed" Air pollution , for example, accounts for 2.7 million to 3.0 million of deaths annually and of these 90% are from developing countries. " Hence, our societies need to concern human right law to protect unfair treatment to developing countries people. Firstly, both disciplines have deep social root, even though human rights law is more rooted within the collective consciousness, the accelerated process of environmental degradation is generating a new " environmental consciousness". Secondly, both disciplines have become internationalized . The international community has assumed the commitment to observe the realization at human rights and respect for the environment. Thirdly, both areas of law tend to universalize their object of protection. Human rights are presented as universal and the protection of the environment appears as everyone is responsibility.

Human right and environment law can raise our quality of life because the first approach is one where environmental protection is described as a possible means of fulfulling human rights standards. Here, environmental law is conceptualized as giving a protection that would help ensure the well-being of future generations as well as the survival of those who depend immediately upon natural resources for their livelihood. So, the end is fulfulling human rights, and the route is though environmental law, the second approach places the two sphere in inverted positions, it states that the legal protection of human rights is an effective means to achieving the ends of conservation and environmental protection. Therefore, the presently existing human right is as a route to environmental protection. The focus is on the connection to influence any economy: health, food supply , housing, fresh natural air supply etc. aspects of quality of life issues. Hence, human right and environment law and human quality of life and economic growth has close relationship . We can not neglect to concern how to achieve human right law to protect our nature environment existing in our societies.

What are environmental factors affect human health in important way, both positive and negative? On positive environmental factor aspect, which can sustain health, and promoting them is preventive medicine. They include : sources of nutrition (farming, oil quality, water availability, bio diversity/bio integrity, genetically modified organisms ; hurting, fishing: wildlife, fish populations; water (drinking, cooking, cleaning,sanitation); air quality; ozone layer (protection from cancers disease etc).; space for exercise and recreation, sanitation/waste recycling and disposal. On negative environmental factors aspect, which are threats to health, and controlling them is public environmental health. They include: environmental conditions favouring disease sectors (endemic and exotic sectors); invasive biota (visuses, bacteria etc.), their hosts and sectors; environmental disruptions: floods, droughts, storms, fires earthquakes, volcanoes; air quality: pollution landing to respiratory disease or cancers; water quality: biotic and abiotic contaminants ; integrity of water transport and intrastructure; monitoring and management of municipal, agricutural, industrial outflows to the environment (gases, liquids, solid waste), human changes of the environment that: create conditions that favour disease; disturb and release noxious levels of previously bound chemicals (e.g. mercury released becomes poison) or bioto (e.g. methane released from thawed peat contributes to climate changes, create temporary, intense, life threatening heat islands (e.g. urban heat waves exacerbated by climate change); result from nuclear; biological or chemical welfare or terrorism, disruption cased by other war and violense. So, it implies , such as India developing county, which have large population are living in this country and their health is bad, due to air and water pollution is serious. So, environmental protective product needs will have more.

What is space and environmental technology?

For example, Cananda is a developed country and it begins to concern environmental pollution challenge to announced $3 million to support the initiative strengthening health and environment linkages: from knowledge to action. The initiative will bring together scientific, technical and socio-economic information on environment and health linkages, and transfer that knowledge to inform decision-making at the local, regional and national levels. Also, Canada is principally concerned with the health of Canadians. This involves health factors in Canada and in biologically shared health regions (shared geography or exposure through trade and travel). Supports international health initiatives, such as determining health risks throught environmental analysis of disease vectors in Africa or Asia.

How can the space and environmental factors affecting health? Environmental information and environmental management contribution to the maintenance and restoration of health. Space based environmental management factors and communications can play roles in: Environmental information is for optimising use of health resources; distribution of and access to health advice and treatment (i.e. to health staff treatment facilities; short range environmental prediction for avoidance of high risk, situations and to guide immediate health system responses. Managing acute risks, adopting to them (e.g. temporary moving of vulnerable elderly monitored; modeling of health impact of environmental parameters; prediction of long term health resource needs and environmental planning and mitigation and adaptation to global changes. Large benefits are possible from attention to environmental factors, e.g. asthma prevention, disease and epidemiology. Benefits need to be quantified. This is of particular interest and relevance to pandemics , such as malasia in underdeveloped countries, potentially saving thousands of lives.

What is space and environmental technology? It can contribute to and keep abreast of environmental health forecasts (using existing models and known parameters); prepare and deliver prospectuses for what space can do in anticipation or response; steer space programs according to real risks and real accumulative health benefits, as long technical investment, don't focus primarily on threats that may have high emotional impact , but are of low actual risk; position space technology and the canadian space program in people's winds, aggressively and realistically, as a first line contributor to foresight and preduction, long term maintenance of well-being and prevention of factors of ill-health ; ongoing delivery of health services and management of current health factors and potentially capable and ready to respond in health emergencies. Finally, making the full business case for environmental protective product investment in space technology and space program contributions relative to the full and public and private cost of health programs. This connects not only to GDP raising, but to indicators of quality of life to any countries.

Why does environment protective product need survey to enquire design questions?

In conclusion, environment protective product researchers are similar to design product researchers who can use interviews and questionnaires to measure consumer response to their both products? They have similar point, such as environment protective products and general products which need to be designed. If the design of environment protective product is very attractive to compare other environment protective product competitors. Then, its sale numbers have possible to be increased. Hence, face to face walking interview and questionnaires with pedestrians is one kind of consumer behavior prediction method.

In psychology view point, implications tests have been developed in an attempt to overcome and to obtain investigates the adaptation of implicit methods to measure how to design product preference. Two questions are for test. (I) establishing an acceptable methodology for tests using environment protection product images . (ii) determining whether response to design environment protection products can produce significant effects in affective experiments.

How can environment protection design researchers predict how to design their environment protectionproduct to be more attractive? Understanding how environment protection consumers experience to design environment protection products have important implications for environment protection design research and design practice. These questions are often investigated experimentally by presenting consumers with a range of environment protection products or design variants and measuring subjective response for future design development. Measuring environment protection consumer response to design environment protection product testing, e.g. survey methods, questionnaires, interviews and focus groups. Questionnaire methods are especially popular, and often feature attitude response, such as choice questions. Although, those explicit measures can provide helpful feedback to environment protection product designers, who are also subject to a number of limitations. Consumer survey responses to a product or predict future environment protection behavior, such as how to design environment protection product purchasing decisions in the environment protection marketplace.

In some cases, environment protection participants might be motivated to answer a questionnaire dishonestly, or in a way that seems most socially acceptable. However, the survey may not be targeting the same thought processes that a consumer faces in the environment protection product use scenario or in the environment protection marketplace. There is evidence that actual environment protection product-related behavior is affected by more spontaneous or processes, as consumers are often distracted or pressed for time when consuming actual environment protection products or making purchasing decisions. Other methods include psychophysiological techniques, such as eye tracking, brain imaging, heart rate measurement, and voice pitch analysis for an overview of these methods applied to design environment production product measuring to consumer responses.

Can implicit design questionnaire (survey) or /and interview methods can test consumer behavior for measuring consumer response to environment protection product?

Some design researchers often use interviews and/or questionnaires to measure consumer response to any product design method, such as environment protection product. In psychology, " implicit" tests have been developed in an attempt to overcome self-report biases and to obtain a more automatic measure of attitudes. Two exploratory studies have conducted to (i) establishing an acceptable methodology for implicit tests using product images, and (ii) determining whether response to products can produce significant effects in affection.

How to contribute design-research methodological developments for measuring consumer response. For example, product design research and conventional methods need to be gathered consumer feedback. How can consumer research in product design? Understanding how consumer experience designed products has important implications for design research and design practice. Thus, product manufacturers need to attempt to develop knowledge about the relationship between product designs and the responses who elicit from consumers, e.g. borrowing which product features can contribute to consumer preference by presenting consumers with a range of products or design variants and measuring subjective responses to them. This process can offer guidance for what products or design variants might be most preferred and can give useful clues for further design development.

Consumer response can be measured by questionnaires(surveys), interviews and focus groups. Questionnaire methods are especially popular and often feature attitude response. However, consumer survey responses may not fully capture reactions to a product or predict future behavior, such as purchasing decisions in the marketplace. This is evidence that actual product-related behavior is affected any more spontaneous or impulse processes , as consumers are often distracted or processes for time when consuming products or making product decisions (Friese, Hofman & Wanke, 2009). For example, cell phone images can be replaced with cars in order to develop the experiment using a second product category. As with phones, vehicles were chose , due to their wide appeal, user involvement and variety of models for potential testing.

In these experimental studies, the consumption psychologists selected products from two categories (phone models and car models) with the intention of measuring significant differences in approach bias among product stimuli. These consumption psychologists aim to test that of the method could be defined to measure attitudes with sufficient sensitivity, variants of particular designs could also be used as stimuli, offering feedback on the viability of different design directions. The consumption psychologists feel it will be helpful to add multiple questions to the self-report stage . Instead of a single attractiveness rating, who might as about " liking" or "employing additional methods". Comparison with real would measure , such as willingness to pay, prior ownership or observed consumption behavior may also be instructive. It may also be worthwhile test a version of the task where the correct response is determined by a feature, such as class membership (product color), shape, brand etc. instead of image ,location or rotation. It seems survey method can be used to predict whether how to design environment protection product to attract many consumer choices. In the economic view point, instead of consumer will compare different similar product price, who also compare product color, shape, size of design factor to decide to make final consumption decision.

www.ingramcontent.com/pod-product-compliance
Lightning Source LLC
Chambersburg PA
CBHW060216120726
48004CB00008B/1834